ON NOT BEING SOMEONE ELSE

On Not Being Someone Else

Tales of Our Unled Lives

ANDREW H. MILLER

Harvard University Press

Cambridge, Massachusetts
London, England

Copyright © 2020 by the President and Fellows of Harvard College
All rights reserved
Printed in the United States of America

First Harvard University Press paperback edition, 2022
First printing

Library of Congress Cataloging-in-Publication Data
Names: Miller, Andrew H., 1964– author.
Title: On not being someone else : tales of our unled lives / Andrew H. Miller.
Description: Cambridge, Massachusetts : Harvard University Press, 2020. |
Includes bibliographical references and index.
Identifiers: LCCN 2019054803 | ISBN 9780674238084 (cloth) |
ISBN 9780674271180 (pbk.)
Subjects: LCSH: Self in literature. | Existentialism in literature. |
Identity (Psychology) in literature.
Classification: LCC PN56.S46 M55 2020 | DDC 809/.93353—dc23
LC record available at https://lccn.loc.gov/2019054803

For Mary

CONTENTS

We saw for a moment laid out among us the body of the complete human being whom we have failed to be, but at the same time cannot forget. All that we might have been we saw; all that we had missed, and we grudged for a moment the other's claim, as children when the cake is cut, the one cake, the only cake, watch their slice diminishing.

—VIRGINIA WOOLF, *THE WAVES*

PREFACE

When asked by a reporter whether being rich had made him happy, Neil Diamond is said to have replied that money hadn't made much of a difference in his life. "You can only spend so much money," he said. "What are you going to do? Have two lunches?"

―――――――

Asked to describe myself, I might say many things. I might say I'm a teacher or a writer, I might describe my habits or my looks, I might mention my family or the town in which I live, or the town from which I came. In any case, I would probably talk about who I am. But sometimes I think about myself in a very different way, focusing not on who I am but on who I'm not. I think about the lives I might have led, the people I might have become, had things gone differently in the past. Each of us no doubt could make a list: if my parents hadn't moved from Connecticut when I was young; if I had gone to a different college; if I hadn't taken that one class with that one teacher; if my girlfriend hadn't broken up with me; if my parents hadn't gotten a divorce; if I had taken another job; if my wife and I hadn't had children. . . . What would my life be like? What would I be like?

There are an unending number of lives I'm not leading, so why do I fixate on this one or that one? Why is *this* life the one I care about not living? I'm not a podiatrist, not a landscape designer, can't play the flute, and haven't married a Canadian. I don't live in Kansas. So what? These things don't chafe my spirit—they never occur to me. That I'm not as generous as my wife, as smart as my friend, as funny as my brother; that I'm not young. . . . These thoughts live with me, and when I leave the house they come along. When I tell you who I am not, I tell you who I am.

It's true that I may not be telling you *much* about who I am. I stand slump-shouldered on the wet sidewalk as the bus lifts away, carrying with it that other me, the one who didn't stop in the doorway of Macy's to fish a pebble from his shoe, and who now sits in comfort, retrieving his phone from his pocket and wedging the earbuds into his ears. But the bus turns the corner and he's gone. And in any case, I don't need an unsoaked alter ego to tell me I'm impatient and don't like getting caught in the rain. At other times, though, my imagined selves linger longer and say more. In the pages to come, I let them linger, and listen to what they say.

The philosopher Bernard Williams calls the thought that I might have been someone else "very primitive." He means that it's a fundamental, basement-level thought, a thought about what it is to be a person at all. But it's so fundamental that we often overlook it; we build other thoughts on top of it, and so hide it. When Williams goes on to call this thought "very real," then, it's with an air of insistence, as if he needed to remind himself that it's true. This combination of obviousness and obscurity makes unled lives hard to write about. Sometimes my thoughts have seemed to resonate more deeply than I could say; at other times, they've seemed too dull to write down. No wonder, given the difficulties, that I've turned to literature. Psychologists and philosophers have studied unled lives, but creative writers know them best. These lives trouble the way language ordinarily works—trouble our pronouns, our diction, our syntax, the tone and cadences of our phrases—and writers find their opportunities in our trouble. Indeed, unled lives have given modern literature one of its great themes—or so I hope to show.

Of course, you might say that *all* fictional characters are unrealized possibilities, living lives unled by either writers or their readers: that's what it means to be fictional. "The characters in my novels are my unrealized possibilities," writes Milan Kundera in *The Unbearable Lightness of Being.* "That is why I am equally fond of them all and equally horrified by them. Each one has crossed a border that I myself have circumvented. It is that crossed border (the border beyond which my own 'I' ends) which attracts me most. For beyond that border begins the secret the novel asks about." To the extent that novels give us stories about how things really are, a space opens to tell us how things might have been but are not. And so, too, with plays, films, and poems: they present to us a recognizable reality, but one not entirely ours.

Yet, if all literature and film represented unrealized possibilities, there would be no end of works that I might write about. For a long time, this thought stymied me and I couldn't see a way forward. I found other things to work on. But I kept coming back to these unled lives—or they came back to me. And after a while, I noticed that their stories tended to have a particular shape. It shouldn't have taken me so long: the form is there in one of the most familiar poems there is, Robert Frost's "The Road Not Taken." A traveler pauses to look back at two roads that diverged in the past; now, having taken one of the roads, he compares it with the other. One person, two roads, retrospection, comparison: when I saw that this pattern underlay the poems and novels I had read and the films I had watched, writing this book suddenly seemed possible. New works I encountered—this week a story by Kathleen Collins, the week before that a lyric by Charles Simic, last month a memoir by Cory Taylor and a film by Andrew Haigh—found their places. I saw, too, that works I don't know, but that readers might, would also find their places. I could write, and imagine an end to writing, because I could imagine how readers might continue.

In these stories there are a lot of journeys: characters leave home, drift down streams, take trains, share cabs, fly to new continents. These trips didn't surprise me—these are stories about paths, after all. But other motifs were more puzzling. Early on I noticed that various gods kept showing up, not commanding the stage, perhaps, but hanging around in the wings. Why should this be? And why, I wondered, were these gods so often incompetent? I also wondered why characters in these stories worried so much about whether they were like other people or unique, commonplace or exceptional. It didn't seem to be simply vanity, or solely vanity, but a more rudimentary uncertainty. What does it have to do with the thought that they might have been someone else? And, finally, why are so many of these stories violent? Why are characters so often mutilated, murdered, annihilated? Why, even when the stories are bloodless, should their language be so extreme? *All* the difference? Caused by the choice of a road? Really?

These motifs and the simple shape of Frost's poem organize this book. After an introduction, the first section describes the form taken by stories of unled lives, focusing on its two central features: the thought that you're only one person and the thought that your life has been shaped by a fork in your road. In the second section I consider the social and historical conditions that encourage this way of thinking. No doubt that when the wind slackened and the sun stood still, Odysseus had some second thoughts, and Job, too, might have found things to regret. But the number of people we are not, like the number of people we are, has grown in recent centuries. For some modern authors, unled lives have drawn on their deepest motivations and allowed them to write about what matters most to them. These writers—among them Charles Dickens, Henry James, Thomas Hardy, Virginia Woolf, and Philip Larkin—will turn up often in the pages to come. Others have written about unled lives more intermittently, as if in response to a nagging perplexity. I discuss their work, too, hoping to make plausible my claim that unled lives are a major theme of modern literature. Though I take no census—the demographics would be tricky—I'm sure that unled lives remain on the rise today. For a while I kept a list of contemporary writers and directors whom I might include in this book, a list that started with the novelist Kate Atkinson and ended with the poet Rachel Zucker: Paul Auster, Nicholson Baker, Julian Barnes, Noah Baumbach, Jesse Browner, Lucille Clifton, Michael Cunningham, Rachel Cusk. . . . But the list soon became unwieldy and I gave it up. Why should so many people today care about the people they are not?

Finally, in the third section, I consider the feelings that come with these stories. What emotions lead us to imagine our unled lives? And what emotions do those lives lead us to? That I feel regret and, sometimes, relief as I read about them didn't surprise me. Nor did my envy or sympathy. But I have other feelings, too, harder to locate and to name. Why do I sometimes feel queasy, as if I have nausea or vertigo? Why at the same time, do I often find myself laughing? And why, at other times, do I feel so delicate and deep a tenderness? Thinking about the unrealized possibilities living in his books, Kundera felt both horror and fondness. My feelings, too, have been a strange mix of the sharp and sweet, extreme and mild.

To balance my brisk movement from poem to short story to novel to film and back to another poem, I've punctuated the large sections with three interludes, each focused on a single work: Carl Dennis's "The God Who Loves You," Frank Capra's *It's a Wonderful Life*, and Ian McEwan's *Atonement*. Choosing different sorts of work—a poem, a film, a novel—lets me consider the resources and limitations of different genres. Fiction may be the natural home for the people we are not, but as Frost's inescapable poem suggests, they also flourish in poetry—something that *It's a Wonderful Life* suggests for film as well. Unlived lives have pressed artists to explore the resources of their mediums. I expect that this challenge is part of what appealed to them. It's appealed to me, too. Whatever its limits, criticism has its resources, and I've used them as best I can to understand the lives we haven't led and the literature that illuminates those lives. This organization makes for a loose-limbed essay, but one orderly enough, I hope, that readers will see ways to go forward, and promising enough that they will want to.

Of course, in writing a book about unled lives you think about books unwritten—all the ideas you might have included, all the directions you could have taken, all the material you've left behind in electronic folders unlikely ever to be opened again. I say little about the importance of my theme in different national literatures. I suspect that it's more common in British than in American or Continental writing, but I'm not sure. I say less about film than I would like, and nothing about drama or music. (I don't think Neil Diamond sang about unlived lives, but Tom T. Hall did in his perfectly pitched song "Pamela Brown": "I'm the guy who didn't marry pretty Pamela Brown / Educated, well-intentioned, good girl in our town. / I wonder where I'd be today if she had loved me too. / Probably be driving kids to school." It's a plangent bit of irony: "I guess I owe it all," he says, "to Pamela Brown.") I thought that I would write more about sexuality, but have found less than I expected. I look at stories about racial passing, but not much at race beyond that. I draw on the work of philosophers, but don't really argue for many theses. I say little about the relation between looking back to past opportunities and forward to future ones, nothing about the relation of alternate lives to alternate history, nothing about doubles and doppelgängers . . . and so on. My belief that I've identified something new and in need of more thought than I can give it has been the justification I've given myself for these various omissions. As it is, I've had enough on my hands to answer the questions I've chosen: Why are writers so interested in that elusive, inescapable creature whom Woolf called "the complete human being whom we have failed to be, but at the same time cannot forget"? Why am I?

However much money you have, you can only have one lunch, and here it is, on the table in front of you. But, of course, there were other lunches on the menu, other lunches you might have ordered. The restaurant is busy. Waiters thread through the room, carrying plates clouded in steam, sliding them in front of others at your table, others across the room. Fork in hand, you pause and look around.

ON NOT BEING SOMEONE ELSE

Introduction

One's real life is so often the life that one does not lead.

—OSCAR WILDE, "ENVOI"

I've become accustomed, if not happily accustomed, to thinking of my life as having a beginning and an end. I'm traveling down a path; I started one day and one day I'll stop. But paths, like pages, have margins, and these margins mark limits, too. It isn't just that my life will come to an end, be limited in the future, but that it's limited *now*: I have one life, this one. Not only will I have no life after this one, I have no life other than this one. I'm no one but myself. You'd think this would be obvious enough. Why, then, does it sometimes strike me as a revelation? There are so many other paths I might have taken, so many other lives I might have led, and yet I find myself here, on this fresh June day, a middle-aged man in Baltimore, behind this narrow desk, looking out at those two children playing on the shaded sidewalk under the dogwood trees as I write these words for an unknown audience. . . . What are the odds?

I'm so intimate with myself, and alone in that intimacy. No one else has my memory of running back through the just-blooming forsythia bushes, across the Richmonds' field on that early spring evening, chased by a friend, feeling the tightening pain in my calf, laughing and stumbling, lashed by the bending branches. . . . Such experiences *are* me, I want to say. Yet they could have been so different, I could have been so different. And there has been an infinity of such moments, any one of which could have sent me stumbling off in a direction different from the one that has led me here, now, to this city, this house, this room, this desk, this sentence. A life so unlikely, yet so inescapable.

———

The thought that I might have become someone else is so bland that dwelling on it sometimes seems fatuous—a making much out of nothing. But I think there's a real puzzle here, even if it's hard to keep steadily in focus. A comparison may help. In 1913, Sigmund Freud and Rainer Maria Rilke took a summer walk through the countryside in the Dolomites. Rilke was unhappy, Freud tells us, depressed by the thought that the beauty around him was doomed. "It would vanish," the poet said, "when winter came, like all human beauty." This was a typically gloomy remark; several years later, Rilke would call happiness "that over-hasty profit from imminent loss," and would describe mankind this way:

> Us, the most transient.
> Everyone *once, once* only. Just *once* and no more.
> And we also *once.* Never again.

Freud didn't share Rilke's despair. The knowledge that the things of this world will pass away doesn't diminish their beauty, he thought. On the contrary: any "limitation in the possibility of an enjoyment raises the value of the enjoyment." This was a brave idea much in the air during those years, as Europe headed toward the battles of World War I. It was in 1915 that Wallace Stevens would write, "Death is the mother of beauty."

As they took their walk, Freud and Rilke were discussing our mortality and the ways it affects the pleasure we take in the beauty of the world. Does death drain the world of beauty, they asked, or does it distill that beauty? But this is exactly what I'm *not* interested in. I'm interested in something more elusive, but no less fundamental: not our mortality but our singularity. The plea from the heart here is not "Everyone *once, once* only," but "Everyone *one, one* only." This singularity shapes our experience of ourselves and of the world around us no less than does our mortality. Of course, the two are related. The thought that I'll die makes me feel more sharply the fact that I'm living only one life now. "Once the next life—the better life, the fuller life—has to be in this one, we have a considerable task on our hands," writes the psychologist Adam Phillips. "Now someone is asking us not only to survive but to flourish, not simply or solely to be good but to make the most of our lives. It is a quite different kind of demand. The story of our lives becomes the story of the lives we were prevented from living."

It's a familiar thought that art responds to our mortality—defends against it, attempts to transcend it, comes to terms with it. But art also, equally, responds to our singularity.

———

When I tell people I'm writing about the lives we haven't led, they usually bring up "The Road Not Taken." I nod and shuffle the conversation along, a bit embarrassed. I worry that Frost's poem will prove that I've been preoccupied with something we already know all about. But for all its well-fingered familiarity, "The Road Not Taken" remains a mysterious piece of writing, spare and extreme:

> Two roads diverged in a yellow wood,
> And sorry I could not travel both
> And be one traveler, long I stood
> And looked down one as far as I could
> To where it bent in the undergrowth;
>
> Then took the other, just as fair,
> And having perhaps the better claim,
> Because it was grassy and wanted wear;
> Though as for that the passing there
> Had worn them really about the same,
>
> And both that morning equally lay
> In leaves no step had trodden black.
> Oh, I kept the first for another day!
> Yet knowing how way leads on to way,
> I doubted if I should ever come back.
>
> I shall be telling this with a sigh
> Somewhere ages and ages hence:
> Two roads diverged in a wood, and I—
> I took the one less traveled by,
> And that has made all the difference.

Frost's tone is mild, but his thought is extravagant: to be sorry you can't be one traveler on two roads—to be sorry you can't be two places at once—is to be sorry for what you are, for what we are. It's to be sorry for being a person. "The Road Not Taken" is a

poem of metaphysical resignation, of sorrow at our inevitable re-
linquishments. And yet this very large sorrow was prompted by
something very small, merely a fork in the woods, leading to two
roads "about the same." From such slight, perhaps imperceptible,
perhaps nonexistent differences, *all* the difference has followed.
Consequences are disproportionate to their causes.

For all his calm assurance, Frost's speaker seem oddly uncertain about the choice he made. Were the roads the same or not?
Was one more worn than the other? It's unclear. But this traveler
does know that the choice he made that day made a difference: it
has meant everything for him. He also evidently knows how
"way leads on to way" and knows that his way will lead him at
some point in the future to tell a story about his choice and its
effects—and, of course, he's telling such a story now in the poem
itself. Though way leads on to way, leading away, though he can't
return to his past, his words can retrace his journey.

As if to insist on this power of words, Frost himself returns
near the end of his poem to where he started. "Two roads diverged
in a yellow wood," he began, and now he says: "Two roads diverged in a wood." This is only one of several phrases varied or
repeated in the poem. Another comes at the poem's emotional
peak a beat later:

> Two roads diverged in a wood, and I—
> I took the one less traveled by

When I read these lines aloud, I feel his feelings choked in the
back of my throat: whatever difference his choice made is held unsaid in a stutter. "I—/I": the speaker is a dash and a line break
away from himself. This doubled "I" makes a fitting climax for a
poem that's been shaped by repetition from its start. The word

"and" opens three lines in the first stanza, and opens others in the second and third, and then returns to open the poem's final line: one thing and another and another. Each time a new "and" appears, I take another step along the poem's way. And yet, each time I hear the word, my ears remember all the earlier "ands." As I move forward, I bring what I've read with me. I'm like the speaker, who can't leave the past even as he steps into the future.

Such reversals are the business of verse; poems become themselves by returning to themselves. But why should a poem that begins with a choice between roads end with a tale being told? What's the relation between unrealized possibilities and the stories we tell? These are my questions, tucked within Frost's poem.

———

"Long I stood," Frost's speaker tells us. Before anything else, before we imagine ourselves as solitary and our past divided, before we have our feelings and thoughts, we need time for thought. Two friends sit before a fire, a husband talks to his wife at day's end, one person is stuck in traffic on the way home from work and another is stuck after grocery shopping. A woman takes a break to mend a dress, a fast-moving train pulls into a station, a man looks out the window on his way from bed to the bathroom, a young girl sits for fifty minutes with her analyst. One way or another, a recess for reflection is found in the day. We become still, look out from where we are, and see where we're not. This is a description of reading, too, of course. Silently, at an uncertain distance, these characters give us emblems of ourselves.

———

Stories of lives unled encourage some ways of thinking and feeling and discourage others; they raise some questions and hide others, they amplify some experiences and silence others. We needn't think of life this way, and we often don't. Picture your life for a moment not as a forking path but as a card game. You had this opening or that, depending on how others played, and you played well or played poorly. In this way, the picture of life as a game, like that of a forking path, invites you to think about the choices you've made and the luck that has befallen you. Maybe you shot the moon, maybe you came annihilatingly close. But the metaphor of the card game also encourages you to think about the conditions of your life. What hand were you dealt?

In drawing my attention to the possibilities I've encountered along my path, stories of unled lives lead me away from questioning the conditions into which I was born. (They're ethical stories, perhaps, before political ones.) Or, rather, they lead me to look at one fundamental condition, that of being this single self among many possible selves. They focus my attention on sharp, particular sensations: the smell of the hospital, the name of the nurse, the look on his face. And at the same time, they focus my attention on airy, abstract ideas: being one person among all the people I might have been. Attention so divided can break and remake language.

––––––––––

"One of the most significant facts about humanity," writes the anthropologist Clifford Geertz, "may finally be that we all begin with the natural equipment to live a thousand kinds of life but end in the end having lived only one." Or as the poet and critic William Empson put it more briefly, "There is more in the child than any man has been able to keep." While growth realizes, it narrows: plural possibilities simmer down into one reality, haloed by evaporating, airborne unrealities. There's loss to be found, if

you look, in the bare fact that you've had only one past and arrived at only one present. Life is *exclusive*. If this can be said about
life it can be said, too, about stories—can be said about both
because we so often think of our lives *as* stories. "In the beginning" of a story, writes Paul Goodman, "anything is possible; in
the middle things become probable; in the ending everything is
necessary." Growth excludes and *hardens*. Or so it can seem.

————

"The Road Not Taken" is the classic poem of unled lives, the
first of many we'll read. Poems have practical advantages. When
they're short, they can be quoted complete, which allows more
authoritative, and so more valuable, disagreement. You'll measure your distance from me more surely if you can see the ground
between us. Completeness has a theoretical value, too, for it's
when an experience is over that I'm most inclined to imagine it
otherwise.

But there's another reason that I've turned to poetry. Poems
create with special power the experience of *verging* on meaning:
something important is being said, but what isn't clear. You're
in the presence of meaning, but don't possess it. For some tem-
peraments—for my temperament—this experience is endlessly
seductive. Meaning may never come, and that may be fine. (I think
of T. S. Eliot's remark that "the chief use of the 'meaning' of a
poem, in the ordinary sense, may be . . . to satisfy one habit of the
reader, to keep his mind diverted and quiet, while the poem does
its work upon him: much as the imaginary burglar is always provided with a bit of nice meat for the house-dog.") But if you do
find a meaning, if the poem does gain weight for you, that meaning
will be inseparable from what led to it; the experience of reading
the poem remains within whatever you take away. For a critic, this

makes interpretive tact important: like a good teacher, you need to know what to leave unsaid, and when to stop.

———

Psychologists have wondered why it is that we should ever engineer our own regret. It's true that we sometimes imagine worse unreal lives for ourselves and so are relieved to be living our real one: there but for the grace of god go I, we say. But more often than not, we imagine a better past for ourselves and feel regret. The explanation many psychologists give for this is resolutely practical: when we think things have gone wrong, we imaginatively improve upon the past so that we might not make the same mistake in the future. Some give this self-training an evolutionary cast: "Enhanced processing following negative outcomes that permits the avoidance of future negative outcomes has obvious survival value," as Neal Roese and James Olson put it.

But this is a dreary picture of our many-shaded motivations. It's not, first of all, to permit the avoidance of future negative outcomes that we create unled lives, but to find meaning in the life we do lead. The need for a meaningful life comes before any calculation, and contemplating lives we haven't led is an especially powerful way of making or finding that meaning.

———

Fiction, like poetry, can create this experience of verging on meaning, but its length makes it less convenient for a critic. Plot summary and long quotations are inevitable. Still, unled lives thrive in fiction, and so it's with fiction—and novels especially— that I'll spend much of my time. Unled lives are coded deeply in the novel's DNA and have been since the beginning. Stranded on his island, Robinson Crusoe looks around him. He compares his

situation, bleak enough, with what it would have been had his ship
not been near the shore when it foundered, and had he not been
able to retrieve his tools and weapons from it. He spends whole
days, he says, picturing "in the most lively colours, how I must
have acted if I had got nothing out of the ship." At this symbolic
moment of origin—for Crusoe, for the novel—speculation about
what hasn't happened established a secure beachhead. And as
novels advanced through the culture, so did this sort of speculation, taking firmer hold in the nineteenth and then the twentieth
century. In stories by Jane Austen, Charles Dickens, George Eliot,
Thomas Hardy, Virginia Woolf, Zora Neal Hurston, Phillip Roth,
Mary Gordon, Lionel Shriver, Colum McCann, Elena Ferrante,
and many others, unlived lives found their due amplitudes of
implication.

———

If Frost's "The Road Not Taken" is the classic poem of unlived
lives, Henry James's "The Jolly Corner" is the classic story.

Decades ago, Spencer Brydon gave up his life in New York City
and traveled to Europe, where he "followed strange paths and
worshiped strange gods," living what he calls a selfish, frivolous,
scandalous life. Now middle-aged, he's returned to New York to
look after the two houses he owns there, and has taken up with
an old friend, Alice Staverton. One day, as the pair sit in her
modest home, Brydon remarks that for him, now, all things "come
back to the question of what he personally might have been, how
he might have led his life and 'turned out,' if he had not so, at the
outset, given it up"—given up, that is, a life in New York:

> What would it have made of me, what would it have made
> of me? I keep forever wondering, all idiotically; as if I could

possibly know! I see what it has made of dozens of others, those I meet, and it positively aches within me, to the point of exasperation, that it would have made something of me as well. Only I can't make out what, and the worry of it, the small rage of curiosity never to be satisfied, brings back what I remember to have felt, once or twice, after judging best, for reasons, to burn some important letter unopened. I've been sorry, I've hated it—I've never known what was in the letter.

Brydon's curiosity about the unopened letter of his unlived life soon consumes him. He becomes not merely more absorbed in who he is than in anyone else, but more absorbed in who he is not than in anyone else—including Alice. He decants his vanity and serves it to her sediment-free. "Do you believe, then—too dreadfully!—that I *am* as good as I might ever have been?" he asks her, aghast. Evidently, only the best of lost opportunities will do. She replies to this rather recherché anxiety with grace learnt, one suspects, over a lifetime of intelligent deference: "Oh no! Far from it!" But the great thing, she remarks, "seems to me to be that it has spoiled nothing"—that is, Brydon's decision decades ago to travel to Europe has not kept him from arriving here, at her fireplace, with her. Brydon isn't thick: he notices that Alice may be saying something about her feelings for him. But he remains more ardently devoted to the man he is not than to the woman she is.

As if in explanation of his neglect, Brydon tells Alice that she is "a person whom nothing can have altered. You were born to be what you are, anywhere, anyway: you've the perfection nothing else could have blighted." Brydon says this with his characteristically starched condescension: if she couldn't have been otherwise, then there's no interesting story to hear about her. He, fascinatingly, might have been any of many things; she could only ever be what she always has been. And, in fact, James himself tells us next to nothing about Alice—very little about her past or about her present. We mainly learn of her tireless sympathy with Brydon. So, is it Brydon who is neglecting her, or James? Perhaps James, too, thought that a life without alternatives would be a life without a story.

For all Brydon's exquisite narcissism, this quiet scene before the fire is ordinary enough: two old friends turn over the past between them. But as the story continues, its events grow more peculiar. Brydon soon becomes convinced that one of his two houses—the one on the "jolly corner"—actually encloses the world that "might have flourished for him had he not, for weal or woe, abandoned it." Within that other world, he comes to believe, lives the man he would have been had he not left for Europe all those years ago. He begins to haunt his own house: evening after evening in the gathering dusk, he walks to the jolly corner, pulls the door shut behind him, and hunts for the person he hasn't become through the house in which he hasn't lived. When, at last, in the light of a coming dawn, Brydon confronts his prey, the cornered creature is described in meticulous detail: his head is grizzled, and he stands rigid in evening dress, with a dangling double eyeglass, pearl buttons, a gold watch guard, a gleaming silk lappet and white linen. Two of his fingers are mutilated, mere stumps, but this seems only to make him more imposing. So imposing, in fact, that Brydon faints.

With this, we arrive at the story's climax. And yet, what we've been reading remains unclear. For all the bulked description of Brydon's alter ego, it's uncertain whether he really exists—or, rather, it's uncertain how he exists. Are we supposed to think that Brydon swooned before a creature really out there in the world, or before the unreal offspring of his imagination? Are we reading a ghost story, haunted by an actual, if supernatural, creature? Or is this a realistic story of one unhinged man's strange fantasy? James poises the metaphysical and the psychological with expert ambiguity. He's so elaborately reserved, the ample face of his prose so composed, that his intentions are hard to gauge. Unsure what we're reading, unsure what to think or feel, we're made queasy, like Brydon.

When he awakens, Brydon finds his head pillowed in Alice's lap: she dreamt that he was to confront his alter ego that night, became worried, and came to find him. The story then closes with a shuttling exchange between the couple in which Brydon continues to ask the questions that have haunted him: Could I actually have become something like this man? Is this creature truly a possible self of mine? Now, having seen the man, Brydon dreads the thought: "This brute, with his awful face—this brute's a black stranger. He's none of *me*, even as I *might* have been." When Alice replies, "Isn't the whole point that you'd have been different?" Brydon is appalled: "As different as *that* ?" For riches and power, would Brydon have allowed himself to become brutalized? For all the eerie atmosphere of James's story, it's a familiar question. Every day people do terrible things; were I in their place, with their history, would I have done any differently? The person I might have been informs on me not only by confessing my desires but also by revealing my capacities.

Humbled by the discovery of what he doesn't have, Brydon finally sees what he does have: the company of this woman sitting perceptively, receptively, before him. By the end of his story Brydon has returned from his strange travels: "He had come back, yes,—come back from further away than any man but himself had ever traveled; but it was strange how with this sense what he had come back *to* seemed really the great thing, and as if his prodigious journey had been all for the sake of it." He's come back to Alice. James leaves Brydon embracing her and the life he has, rather than the life he doesn't have. "He has a million a year," Brydon finally says, but "he hasn't you." To which Alice replies, as she draws him to her breast, "And he isn't—no, he isn't—*you!*"

———

Brydon has come to terms with the one life he has: a mature response. It's welcome enough when it comes, if it comes. But when it comes here, James's story ends: the pursuit of Brydon's unlived life provided "The Jolly Corner" with its energy; when that search is over, his story is over. And so I've found myself back at the questions raised by "The Road Not Taken." Why did that poem about a life unled end with a story being told? And why does this story about a life unled end when that life is left behind? What, exactly, is the connection between the stories I read and the lives I haven't led?

———

In the months during which he wrote "The Jolly Corner," James was also preparing a collected edition of his prose. In the mornings at his house in Sussex, he would work in the garden, ordering and revising his publications and composing prefaces for them. These prefaces describe where each of his stories was conceived, how it grew, what hopes he entertained for it, what setbacks it suffered, how it struggled with this temptation and was helped along by that chance event. James gave each story its own story, as if writing its biography. Together, these prefaces became standard points of reference for modern thought about fiction. They're important points of reference, too, for thought about unled lives.

James was, to put it mildly, a discriminating writer. He picked over his harvest, discarding a great deal, keeping little, using less. Because his stories are so opulently elaborated, it's easy to miss his asceticism. The sentences he wrote followed selections he made— perhaps consciously, perhaps unconsciously—from an incalculable number of possibilities. And it was on this ground of selection that he drove the stake of value: only if we acknowledge what an author has not done can we appreciate what he has. In the preface to his novel *The Spoils of Poynton,* James puts it this way: "Life being all inclusion and confusion, and art being all discrimination and selection, the latter, in search of the hard latent *value* with which alone it is concerned, sniffs round the mass as instinctively and unerringly as a dog suspicious of some buried bone." James unearthed the bone of *Spoils* itself during a Christmas dinner, when a friend happened to mention a mother and son who were at daggers drawn over the son's inheritance of some valuable furniture. Only ten words had been spoken, James tells us, "yet I had recognized in them, as in a flash, all the possibilities of the little drama of my 'Spoils.'" In another flash, however, he saw those possibilities imperiled: continuing her story, James's friend "complacently and benightedly" began to recount what came of the dispute between the unhappy son and mother. James recoiled: an eleventh word, evidently, would be one too many. The dark threat of knowing what actually happened drove the novelist to Jacobean fantasy and iambic pentameter: "It's the perfect little workable thing," James told himself, "but she'll strangle it in the cradle, even while she pretends, all so cheeringly, to rock it; wherefore I'll stay her hand while yet there's time." It was a narrow escape: James fled with the infant story still breathing, as if under his dinner jacket, saved for his own nursing. Together the adoptive father and foundling would travel down the path of art, not life.

As this may suggest—as James's prefaces make clear—unled lives bring with them a particular aesthetic standard. If art is a matter of choosing among possibilities, then a successful work of art is one that further alteration won't improve; it's finished when any change would be for the worse. Although this is an ancient ideal, rooted in Aristotle's *Poetics,* it gathered new appeal in the eighteenth and early nineteenth centuries. Late in his life, the romantic essayist Charles Lamb was reminded of the famously sardonic remark made about *Paradise Lost* by Samuel Johnson: "None ever wished it longer," Johnson had said. Lamb was indignant. "Nor the moon rounder," was his retort. "Why, 'tis the perfectness and completeness of it, which makes us imagine that not a line could be added to it, or diminished from it, with advantage. Would we have a cubit added to the stature of the Medicean Venus? Do we want her taller?"

That art might leave us longing for nothing is an entrancing thought: we would stand free of need. But it brings with it the idea that successful works of art leave the debris of discarded possibilities behind them, like so many cast-off clothes, or lovers. It sees in beauty something lost and makes of loss something beautiful. James liked the pathos of this idea. The critic Alex Woloch points to the preface of *The Wings of a Dove,* where James reflects on his treatment of one character, Mr. Croy. When James started writing, he had great plans for Croy, but in the end Croy's part was quite small. There was more to him than James could keep. Now, with the novel finished, James can't help but think of all that hasn't happened to the man. His powers begin to stir again, and he devises for his character a brief second act.

> Where do we find him, at this time of day, save in a beggarly scene or two which scarce arrives at the dignity of functional reference? He but "looks in," poor beautiful dazzling, damning apparition that he was to have been; he sees his place so taken, his company so little missed, that, cocking again that fine form of hat which has yielded him for so long his one effective cover, he turns away with a whistle of indifference that nobly misrepresents the deepest disappointment of his life. One's poor word of honour has *had* to pass muster for the show. Every one, in short, was to have enjoyed so much better a chance that, like stars of the theatre condescending to oblige, they have had to take small parts, to content themselves with minor identities, in order to come on at all.

In James's story as it was initially conceived, *every* one was to have enjoyed so much better a chance: poor, disappointed Mr. Croy, looking in from the door, stands for all characters. They're all stars settling for small parts.

But what's most striking to me in this passage is how much James sounds like Spencer Brydon: he thinks as much about the stories he hasn't written as about those he has. "Would we have embarked on *that* stream had we known?" he asks himself at one point in the prefaces. "And what mightn't we have made of this one *hadn't* we known!" How, he wonders, "could we have dreamed 'there might be something'" in this idea? And why in this other "didn't we *try* what there might be, since there are sorts of trials (ah indeed more than one sort!) for which the day will soon have passed?" It's as if James had caught the habit of mind from his characters, or they from him. Evidently, readers can catch it, too: after finishing James's prefaces, Virginia Woolf remarked that "one had almost rather read what he meant to do than read what he actually did do."

Usually," writes Susan Sontag, "critics who want to praise a work of art feel compelled to demonstrate that each part is justified, that it could not be other than it is." This suggests that critics think of a successful work of art in the way that Spencer Brydon thinks of Alice Staverton: it is born to be what it is, anywhere, anyhow, with a perfection that could not be blighted. Like Alice too, the work of art evidently defeats desire, or lies beyond desire's demand. We don't want it to anything other than what it is. And yet, Sontag goes on, "every artist, when it comes to his own work, remembering the role of chance, fatigue, external distractions, knows what the critic says to be a lie, knows that it could well have been otherwise." If ideal works of art are like Alice, real ones are like Brydon.

Sontag presents these two ways of understanding art as the views of two different people, critic and artist. We can toggle between them, putting ourselves first in the place of one, and then the other, but they are two distinct perspectives. And yet, as if by some magic, James sometimes seems to offer both views at once; he lets us see simultaneously the achieved work and its unrealized possibilities. This is perhaps "the essence of James's art," writes the French novelist and critic Maurice Blanchot: "each instant to produce the entire work present" and, at the same time, "to make other forms felt, the infinite and light space of the narrative as it could have been." Another critic, Georges

Poulet, similarly speaks of the effect in James of "dilating the real and loading it with all the possibilities he implies. The real is a center surrounded by a luminous halo of possibilities, at once infinite and finite." The imagery of light is telling. What we see in James's work is the thing itself, solid and real, there in front of us on the page, finished. And yet, that page glows with something bright and weightless, something that's come from afar.

When a work of art manages this trick—when it's lit by what it's not—my feelings, too, become luminous. At these moments, I'm reminded not of art's immortality, but of the fact that this particular poem or film, this story or novel, needn't have existed at all. I'm reminded not that it might endure forever, but that it might not have been. Yet, here it is.

———

Physiologists report that our eyes make little leaps as we read, leap and pause, leap and pause. "Saccades" they're called, a French word for a sailboat's spring when the wind catches its sails. This has been my rhythm as I've tried to understand these stories: forward on a reach, resting, looking back, and then scudding forward again. It's the rhythm of reading. And in this way, I've found myself for a third time back at my questions. Frost's poem about lives unled ended with a story being told; Brydon's story ended when he left behind his unled life; and now James, near the end of his career, ruminates about the tales he hasn't told. What, exactly, is the relationship between the lives we haven't led and the stories we read?

One Person, Two Roads

"The God Who Loves You"

All I could never be,
All, men ignored in me,
This, I was worth to God, whose wheel the pitcher shaped.

—ROBERT BROWNING, "RABBI BEN EZRA"

Unled lives, I'm afraid, are a middle-aged affair. To have an unled life, you need to have a life first. And it's when living a different life in the future seems unlikely that you're most likely to recall the untraveled roads of your past. It was midway upon his life's journey that John Cheever found himself pausing in a dark wood, the right road lost:

> In middle age there is mystery, there is mystification. The most I can make out of this hour is a kind of loneliness. Even the beauty of the visible world seems to crumble, yes even love. I feel that there has been some miscarriage, some wrong turning, but I do not know when it took place and I have no hope of finding it.

Cheever came to his despair early: he was around thirty when he wrote this. For others, fifty seems to be about the time for these lonely mysteries. "You come to this place, mid-life," writes Hilary Mantel. "You don't know how you got here, but suddenly you're staring fifty in the face. When you turn and look back down the years, you glimpse the ghosts of other lives you might have led; all houses are haunted." And it's in James's "The Diary of a Man of Fifty" that the narrator realizes that

> there would always remain a certain element of regret; a certain sense of loss lurking in the sense of gain; a tendency to wonder, rather wishfully, what might have been. . . . Why, for instance, have I never married—why have I never been able to care for any woman as I cared for that one? Ah, why are the mountains blue and why is the sunshine warm? Happiness mitigated by impertinent conjectures— that's about my ticket.

You come to this place, Mantel writes, and you don't know how you got there; you pause, like James, and you ask your questions. "By the time they have reached the middle of their life's journey," writes Robert Musil in *The Man Without Qualities*,

> few people remember how they have managed to arrive at themselves, at their amusements, their point of view, their wife, character, occupation and successes, but they cannot help feeling that not much is likely to change anymore. It might even be asserted that they have been cheated, for one can nowhere discover any sufficient reason for everything's having come about as it has. It might just as well have turned out differently.

It *might* have—but it hasn't. And so here you are.

Our culture is famously, excitingly, tediously infatuated with youth, and has been for decades, thick with romantic comedies, young adult novels, bildungsromane. . . . It can seem that youth is the time of stories. But the stories of youth with which we are besotted are, typically, told by older people. They're songs written by the middle-aged and sung as they eye the young. We look back, with whatever feelings, whatever thoughts, to the moment when choices were weighed and hazards risked, before the course of life was set. Neither the liquid choicelessness of childhood nor the frozen choicelessness of middle age, but a world of possibilities, various and new. When we were young, remarks a character in Woolf's *The Waves,* "all simmered and shook; we could have been anything." But now, "change is no longer possible. We are committed. . . . We have chosen now, or sometimes it seems the choice was made for us—a pair of tongs pinches us between the shoulders."

The main figure in Carl Dennis's poem "The God Who Loves You" is driving home from work; it's a dull trip, but its routine emptiness gives him a chance to reflect. Here's how the poem begins:

The God Who Loves You

It must be troubling for the god who loves you
To ponder how much happier you'd be today
Had you been able to glimpse your many futures.
It must be painful for him to watch you on Friday
   evenings
Driving home from the office, content with your week—

Three fine houses sold to deserving families—
Knowing as he does exactly what would have happened
Had you gone to your second choice for college,
Knowing the roommate you'd have been allotted
Whose ardent opinions on painting and music
Would have kindled in you a lifelong passion.
A life thirty points above the life you're living
On any scale of satisfaction. And every point
A thorn in the side of the god who loves you.
You don't want that, a large-souled man like you
Who tries to withhold from your wife the day's
    disappointments
So she can save her empathy for the children.
And would you want this god to compare your wife
With the woman you were destined to meet on the other
    campus?
It hurts you to think of him ranking the conversation
You'd have enjoyed over there higher in insight
Than the conversation you're used to.
And think how this loving god would feel
Knowing that the man next in line for your wife
Would have pleased her more than you ever will
Even on your best days, when you really try.
Can you sleep at night believing a god like that
Is pacing his cloudy bedroom, harassed by alternatives
You're spared by ignorance?

"Have compassion for your guardian angel," the speaker seems
to say—as if this ordinary man stuck in his workday routine could
ease the mind of a fretful god. It's a sly bit of flattery. But we're
not supposed to think there *really* is a god anxiously pacing in

his bedroom; these thoughts are the realtor's thoughts, glorified. In being told to console this downcast divinity, then, the realtor is being told to console himself.

And you're being told to console yourself, too. "It must be troubling for the god who loves you / To ponder how much happier you'd be today / Had you been able to glimpse your many futures." Reading the poem's opening lines, it's natural to assume that you are being addressed—that "you" means you, and that you have an attentive god looking out for you. Another sly bit of flattery. When I was a child and had lost something in the house, a toy or coin, I would think, if there is a god, he knows where my marble rolled, my nickel fell. For a long time, this was the closest I came to god, to his knowledge and his silence. If I could only see from where he sees, or have that special sort of vision he has, I too would know. When I'm dead, I thought, I'll be able to find all my lost things—as if heaven were a last reunion with the lost. As I grew older, I came to think that I could find my lost opportunities there as well. If your god is a loving god, it can be comforting to imagine his or her knowledge of you. In Dennis's poem, the god is comforting in just this companionable way: he knows the realtor, knows what he's done, and knows what he hasn't done. "The death of God," writes Adam Phillips, "is the death of someone knowing who we are."

It's only in reading the next long sentence that you realize that the poet is talking to someone else: a realtor who commutes home from the office on Friday evenings, who went to a particular college, had a particular roommate, and so on. But the trick has done its work: you've been drawn into the poem, invited to see yourself in this man, to participate in his story, even as you recognize your differences. Dennis asks you to reflect on a life which is and isn't yours. Of course, this is what the realtor is doing, too, as he thinks about the life he hasn't led, a life that is and isn't his. And so the unled life that the realtor contemplates as he drives home and the fictional life that you contemplate as you read resonate gently together.

But why has the knowledge of the realtor's lives been displaced onto a *god*? I'll be claiming that unled lives are a largely modern preoccupation. You'd think, then, that all the gods would have absconded. Yet they appear regularly in these stories. In a poem titled "In the Terrible Night," Fernando Pessoa describes a wretched man tormented in bed:

> In the terrible night, natural substance of all nights,
> In the night of insomnia, natural substance of all my
>   nights,
> I remember, awake in tossing drowsiness,
> I remember what I've done and what I might have
>   done in life.
>
> I remember, and an anguish
> Spreads all through me like a physical chill or a fear.
> The irreparable of my past—this is the real corpse.

Trapped in his memories, he thinks,

> what I was not, what I did not do, what I did not
>   even dream;
> What only now I see I ought to have done,
> What only now I clearly see I ought to have been—
> This is what is dead beyond all the Gods.
> This—and it was, after all, the best of me—is what not
>   even the Gods bring to life.

In Emily Dickinson's "Remorse—Is Memory—Awake," the speaker also looks back in the dark. What is remorse? she asks. It is "memory awake . . . Its past set down before the Soul / And lighted with a match / Perusal to facilitate / Of its condensed dispatch."

> Remorse is cureless—the Disease
> Not even God—can heal—
> For 'tis His institution—and—
> The Adequate of Hell.

And in the poem "Lost Days," Dante Gabriel Rossetti sums up his life in a god's company. "The lost days of my life until to-day, / What were they?" he asks.

> I do not see them here; but after death
> God knows I know the faces I shall see,
> Each one a murdered self, with low last breath.
> "I am thyself,—what hast thou done to me?"
> "And I—and I—thyself," (lo! each one saith,)
> "And thou thyself to all eternity!"

These people look back with a bleak fervor: one sees what he ought to have been, another sees the past lit by a match flare, the third sees the faces of his victims. Before anything else, their poems are retrospective. What can they know about the past? How do they feel about it? And how is it connected to the present?

We've already seen the answer to this last question. In the stories we've been looking at, the past and present are connected by a road or track or path or stream down which we can see. This suggests that we can know the past with the immediacy and confidence we ordinarily have with visible things. But, of course, we can't really look at the past, and often have little certainty about it. Sometimes it comes as a confused kaleidoscope of bright, broken colors; sometimes a black and white photograph; sometimes a smell; sometimes it comes as a wave of sourceless feeling running along your skin or through your heavy chest, sometimes it's simply the smile on your face. Rarely do you see it cleanly backlit, as if down an empty road. This, then, is one reason that gods are on hand: they give you an implausible certainty about the life you've led and a more implausible certainty about the lives you haven't.

And yet, there appears to have been an administrative error somewhere: these gods have been issued only half the standard complement of divine powers. They're omniscient, but not omnipotent. Pessoa's dead are dead beyond the gods, Dickinson's god can't heal remorse, and Rossetti's god looks passively at his murdered selves. In their impotence and dubious wisdom, they're figures, maybe a bit hyperbolic, for adulthood. In his novel *A Girl in Winter*, Philip Larkin speaks of a break that comes in most lives, "when the past dropped away and the maturity it had enclosed for so long stood painfully upright." After such a break, he writes, there is "knowledge but no additional strength." The hamstrung divinities that preside over my unled lives dramatize this conflict between the knowledge I seem to have as I look at the past and the power I know I don't have. They keep me company in my informed incapacity.

Dennis's poem also suggests a more psychologically shrewd reason that I imagine pasts for myself. For when I say, if only I had done this or that, things would have been better for me, I can smuggle in, under cover of dark disappointment or darker self-castigation, the assumption that I could have known what to do.

Buyer's remorse, *l'esprit d'escalier,* the feeling I have after I see what others have ordered—"I should have had the duck!"—the whole range of second-guessing moves I make as I try to game my ordinary experience: routine self-criticism nurturing the belief that my life *could* have been perfect. Like Pessoa's speaker, I believe that my unled life was "after all, the best of me." Like Spencer Brydon, I'm vain about my neglected capacities. Failure is merely a falling off from my potential, and heaven a home for my best self. "All I could never be, / All, men ignored in me, / This, I was worth to God, whose wheel the pitcher shaped."

In "The God Who Loves You" Dennis gives this abandoned paradise a name: college. For fortunate Americans, college organizes and institutionalizes the transition from the shapeless play of childhood to the in-box / out-box mechanics of cubicled adulthood: it's a time from which possibilities small and large radiate before we capitulate into maturity. What classes to take, what major to choose, what friends to meet, whom to sleep with, what band to back, what bar to hang out at, whose fake ID to use. . . . The particular possibilities matter less than the feeling of abilities on tap and time to enjoy them; the days, even the boring ones, are full—and there are days and days to come. Or so it can seem, looking back. In "The God Who Loves You," college has set the table for a mess of middle-aged wistfulness.

I know I'm idealizing things. One's twenties can be a time of bewildering disarray and obscure responsibility. For young people now, the choice of a college—if there is a choice—marks the first time they'll have made a big decision with insufficient information. It can also be the first time when implacable social facts—economic facts or facts of social judgment—clang into place to limit choice, to make palpable just how constrained we are. In an instant, the reading of an email message from an admissions office reveals your being, who you are not to yourself or to those you've long known, but to anonymous others presiding over the institutions of adulthood. It can sound like the voice of truth. No longer are you contemplating your place within your family or among people at school; you're contemplating your place among thousands of faceless others. And even if all the admission committees of all the colleges of the world accept you, you can still attend only one school at a time. No wonder that, later, you might want a loving god.

From the vantage of your life now, you look back on your youth. While you might suffer from the memory of past possibilities, you might also welcome their flattery. The realtor's loving god allows him to be warmed by the gilded halo of his unmet potential. If, then, he crowns that god with thorns—if he betrays god's love with his failures—the guilt he suffers is merely the price he pays for keeping faith in his capacities. The more harshly you punish your failures, the more securely you can believe in your exalted potential. You side with your judge and congratulate yourself, righteously or ruefully, on your high standards. Better to identify as a god with a thorn of regret pricking his ribs than to be merely human. And so you strand yourself in perfection. You see what you've done, you see what you could have done, and you know the difference. You know what each event means, and you turn your life into fiction.

That may seem a jump. But one appeal of a loving god lies in the meaning granted by his attention: he makes life entirely meaningful; he makes meaning love's fruit. But this is what narrators do, too: their mere attention confers meaning. No sparrow falls to the ground but they remember it, for they launched it into flight. Simply by including events in their stories, narrators grant them value. And they do this for no reason, gratuitously, impersonally—for you, for me, for anyone Yet, for all that, narrators are powerless over the stories they tell. They have what the critic Elizabeth Ermarth calls "the kind of abstracted and helpless lucidity that succeeds experience." In Christian theology, your guardian angel is also your recording angel, as if recording your life might guard it. As if to be attentively written were not merely to be loved but to be protected. But it's unclear whether this belief lives on in more secular writing.

A picnic has been planned. The guests arrive, the site admired, and a cold collation laid out by unseen servants. Everything is ready for an afternoon's pleasure—yet everyone is dull. The people who have been gathered together want spirit and energy. Soon, our heroine is so bored that when kind, chatty, harmless Miss Bates begins to talk, she can't help herself and ridicules the poor woman. It's excruciating: you've identified with Emma, and now you're stuck with her. In shaming herself, she shames you. And the narrator does absolutely nothing to help. For all that, however, there's gain to be had from this painful scene in Austen's *Emma*. Our understanding of the heroine has been deepened. We now know her better, know her thoughtlessness and her corrigible egotism. The book's meaning has been enriched. If here or there that meaning has seemed paltry—in the unlikely event that Austen's novel, like Miss Bates, seems sometimes empty and dull— then our task is to check again, for the presumption is that meaning is there to be found. If the narrator has included something, it must be meaningful. *Must* be meaningful? Well, that's the presumption. (It was a mark of William Empson's contrariness that he could write to a critic of Hart Crane, "I think your analysis is right as far as it goes, but if completed leaves no word which is at all meaningless.") Reading the sentences of a narrator, you feel not merely that you've gained superhuman knowledge of other people in a fictional world, but that your world, the world outside of the book, might be meaningful to its last detail. This, then, is one hope that the realtor's shadowy god holds out: that your life will reward the sort of close attention you pay to art—the sort of attention I'm asking you to pay to this poem, now.

This is a view of art and life with penetrating appeal—and the speaker of "The God Who Loves You" wants you to give it up. He wants you to let go of the thought that you might be a loving, all-knowing narrator of your own existence. He wants you to let go of the lives you haven't led. Looking back at the opening of the poem, you can see that the speaker has all along been affably mocking toward this "large-souled" realtor. "Three fine houses sold to deserving families...A life thirty points above the life you're living": the realtor's language might as well have come from his house listings, chipper and empty—as if the value of a life, like the value of a house, could be assessed by looking up comps in the neighborhood. Don't use that language, the speaker says: it takes you from yourself. Return to your earth-bound ignorance and find words for it. Here's how the poem continues and concludes:

> The difference between what is
> And what could have been will remain alive for him
> Even after you cease existing, after you catch a chill
> Running out in the snow for the morning paper,
> Losing eleven years that the god who loves you
> Will feel compelled to imagine scene by scene
> Unless you come to the rescue by imagining him
> No wiser than you are, no god at all, only a friend

No closer than the actual friend you made at college,
The one you haven't written in months. Sit down tonight
And write him about the life you can talk about
With a claim to authority, the life you've witnessed,
Which for all you know is the life you've chosen.

In ending "The God Who Loves You" with a plea for letter writing, Dennis returns me again to my guiding thought: unled lives lead to stories. But the story Dennis wants the realtor to tell isn't about a life unled. Instead, it's about the life he has led, the path he has taken. And we're not told that story. It's as if Dennis, like James, were to say that art has little use for our real lives. It was in the other life, after all, the one being dismissed, that the realtor had a passion for art and music. The speaker doesn't say to him, "Write an oratorio about your college life!" or, "Sounds like a good screenplay you've got there!" He says, "Write a letter to a friend."

Yet, what does this poem—intimate, presuming, confiding—resemble but a friend's letter? The casual diction and gentle meter, the end-stopped lines and caesuras that easily accommodate your breath: they all contribute to the informal, unadorned, everyday sound of the voice. It barely seems to be a poem at all. I'm not sure how to think about this. Sometimes, I picture Dennis sitting with a glass of good scotch, canted back comfortably in his chair, reflecting on what he's written, and unconcerned if it isn't everywhere charged with meaning. He seems complacent. But at other times, I think that his artlessness is a real achievement. There's an authority that comes with acceptance, and perhaps the poem in its offhanded ease gives us an image of that acceptance, its grace. Say that it does. How satisfying is it? Do you want it to be other than it is?

Singularity

Every thing is what it is, and not another thing.
—JOSEPH BUTLER, *FIVE SERMONS, PREACHED AT THE ROLLS CHAPEL*

Sitting on her blue sofa, Clarissa Dalloway holds a green dress in her lap. She had been mending it when Peter Walsh burst into the room, back from India, where he's been living for decades, sending her letters she's left unanswered. Now he sits beside her. In the wonder of his appearance, Clarissa finds herself thinking about what would have happened had she married him, as she might have, as he wanted her to, all those years ago. There's a delicate, hovering association between Clarissa's dress and the life she hasn't led with Peter, a soft slant rhyme of slack and empty things.

The thought of life with him leads her to review her real life. An image comes to her. She's walking along the lake near her childhood home, toward her parents who stand in the distance. As she walks, she holds "her life in her arms which, as she neared them, grew larger and larger in her arms until it became a whole life, a complete life, which she put down by them and said, 'This is what I have made of it! This!'" And Peter, having heard Clarissa's voice once more, having remembered their past, having now seen her house, her living room, the inlaid table, the chair covers, the valuable tinted prints—having seen all the things that Clarissa has gathered around her with the man she did marry, Peter feels more intensely his own life, apart from hers. "This has been going on all the time," he thinks: week after week, she has lived her life here while he has lived his, oceans away. Now side by side, they're intimately apart, each enclosed yet close as can be. Though touching, they're separate. To touch they must be separate.

Sometimes my singularity is happy, even delicious. Virginia Woolf—whose novel *Mrs. Dalloway* I've been describing—had a knack for this happiness. In one of her memoirs, she recalls a moment in her childhood when she lay near the sea, half-awake, half-asleep, hearing the waves settle up the shingle. A breeze enters the window, drawing across the floor the acorn that anchors the curtain string. She now looks back and recalls her wonder: that she was alive and was herself in that place, on that day. "If life has a vase that it stands upon," she wrote, "if it is a bowl that one fills and fills and fills, then my bowl without a doubt stands upon this memory." But in less happy moods, singularity can seem a solitary confinement. Woolf had a knack for this feeling, too. I'm trapped within this particular body, these habits, these mannerisms, these ways of speaking and writing, these damn thoughts on this damn day—as if my skin had no pores, my skull no openings. I'm prison and prisoner both. At such moments, the thought of being someone else seems an escape. But who would be escaping? And where would they go?

When I feel myself to be only one person and only this person, other people seem set apart from me. Among others, my singularity becomes separateness. For W. H. Auden, this separateness constituted human suffering:

Musée des Beaux Arts

About suffering they were never wrong,
The old Masters: how well they understood
Its human position: how it takes place
While someone else is eating or opening a window or
   just walking dully along;

How, when the aged are reverently, passionately waiting
For the miraculous birth, there always must be
Children who did not specially want it to happen,
    skating
On a pond at the edge of the wood:
They never forgot
That even the dreadful martyrdom must run its course
Anyhow in a corner, some untidy spot
Where the dogs go on with their doggy life and the
    torturer's horse
Scratches its innocent behind on a tree.

In Breughel's Icarus, for instance: how everything turns
    away
Quite leisurely from the disaster; the ploughman may
Have heard the splash, the forsaken cry,
But for him it was not an important failure; the sun shone
As it had to on the white legs disappearing into the green
Water; and the expensive delicate ship that must have
    seen
Something amazing, a boy falling out of the sky,
Had somewhere to get to and sailed calmly on.

The indifference to others that Auden describes may now be a familiar, anthology emotion. But that indifference rests on a more basic difference: the physical separateness of these creatures. Though they share a moment and a place, each is enveloped in his own body, on the hillside, by the woods, aboard the ship, or slipping into the sea.

———

Auden has taken this scene from Pieter Bruegel's painting *Landscape with the Fall of Icarus*, where irony is a matter of space and scale: the mythic legs are two small strokes, cuticles of flesh in the scalloped waves, drowning in the woozy, foreshortened perspective of the large canvas. Perched awkwardly above his world, Bruegel captured the moment as a photographer might by chance capture tragedy plummeting from above. This is what makes the painting modern, and maybe what made it appeal to Auden. *Landscape with the Fall of Icarus:* even the title makes the fall seem an afterthought. It's as if the painter, like the farmer in the painting, were absorbed in his own task, working on a simple genre scene, when out of the corner of his eye he saw something pale drop downward. He pauses, then joints in a shin and a knee, an inner thigh.

Like Bruegel, Auden measures the distances between the figures he depicts, but he uses a poet's tools. He juxtaposes the diction of extremity with the rhythms of boredom, contrasting "suffering" with the plodding, additive phrasing of "eating or opening a window or just walking dully along." And, again like Bruegel, Auden measures the distance between these figures and himself: he, too, looks on with elevated indifference. This painting, his tone tells us, is merely one masterpiece among many, mattering no more, really, than any of the others.

———

In *The Census at Bethlehem,* hung near *Landscape with the Fall of Icarus* in the Musée des Beaux-Arts in Brussels, Bruegel again paints our separateness: one man bundles branches; another squats, gloves on the snow beside him, to put on his skates; a third taps a keg; a woman sweeps with a broom; another

Pieter Bruegel, *Landscape with the Fall of Icarus*, circa 1558, Royal Museums of Fine Arts of Belgium

Pieter Bruegel, *The Census at Bethlehem*, 1566, Royal Museums of Fine Arts of Belgium

slides forward, wonderfully uncertain, on the ice; yet another feeds the fowl. Each is a marvel of absorption. As the critic Rachel Cohen remarks, Bruegel typically gives each of his figures one action, "done with the body whole"; their concentration encloses them. Even the unmoving have somewhere to get to.

Bruegel has gathered some figures in groups and held others apart. The earth-toned crowd in the lower left-hand corner of the painting draws your eyes first, but there are other, smaller groups: the children sledding, the boy kneeing the toppling girl; the couple at work on the house; the walking companions; the children roughhousing. These figures are joined closely together, but others are separated by caesuras of snow. They rhyme at a distance: two children push themselves along the ice with sticks; two others throw snowballs in different directions; an unevenly spaced trio hunches under similar bundles. Because painting is a spatial medium, Brueghel can do all this casually: there's no fuss in putting one body here and another there, a pair in the distance and a cluster in the foreground.

Gathering people, counting them, noting their occupations: Brueghel is taking his own census. Looking out once more from an awkward upward perch, his attention descends evenly on all. Everyone counts as one—even the woman right of center, riding donkey-back, the woman pregnant with the child some think will save the world. But how should Mary be counted? As one or two? And the child within? Should he count as three? Bruegel's ingenuity lay in seeing the census at Bethlehem as an opportunity to paint our incomprehension of these mysteries. He also saw it as an opportunity to make visible what we can't see—not what lies unseen beyond the frame, but unseen within it. In the stillness of winter, he paints where a painter's counting fails, and his measurements stop: at the feet of the pregnant Mary.

————

But you might say, of course we're separate from each other. Here is one person, and here another. Here I am, there you are. Who ever thought otherwise? One task for painters gripped by this perplexity, then, is to make us feel it for ourselves. They must evoke our separateness if we are to join them as they study it. It's a task for poets and novelists, too, but because their medium isn't spatial, they can't measure physical distances as casually as painters do, nor so casually depict our incomprehension of those distances. That's a limitation, but also an opportunity. For writers have their own resources, their own tools and materials, and they use them to measure distances that aren't spatial. When space evaporates, measurement becomes a matter of comparison, of finding likenesses and differences.

In Browning's "Andrea del Sarto," for instance, the painter rests leisurely and looks back on his career. He holds his life complete. "The whole seems to fall into a shape / As if I saw alike my work and self / And all that I was born to be and do, / A twilight-piece." His thoughts travel to the time he lived at the French court at Fontainebleau. Across a magical year he produced paintings that won the admiration of the king and even "Agnolo," Michelangelo, himself. Each success seemed to issue new promise. "And, best of all," he says, looking at his wife, Lucrezia, who now sits by his side, "this, this, this face beyond, / This in the background, waiting on my work, / To crown the issue with a last reward!" Everything seemed possible: "My youth, my hope, my art" all seemed boundless; surely, he says, I "could sometimes leave the ground, / [And] put on the glory."

"A good time, was it not, my kingly days?" Andrea says to Lucrezia; "and had you not grown restless. . . ." Evidently, it was she who ended Andrea's golden year abroad: "You called me," he says, "and I came home to your heart." But now, years later, she has taken on lovers and lost interest in him; now, he calls her "My moon, my everybody's moon / Which everybody looks on and calls his." Yet Andrea seems no different: he's become an artist for hire, available to anyone who can pay. His painting is merely flawless. And yet, he thinks, it might have been otherwise: had you "given me soul," he says to Lucrezia, "we might have risen to Rafael, I and you!"

> "Live for fame, side by side with Agnolo!
> Rafael is waiting: up to God, all three!"
> I might have done it for you. So it seems:
> Perhaps not.

Browning loved to write deflationary arias like this, which rise in hope then drop into seas of uncertainty. By the poem's end, Andrea can barely sustain routine male passive aggression. He subsides into complacent self-pity. Although the poem's most famous lines—"Ah, but a man's reach should exceed his grasp, / Or what's a heaven for?"—have become an aspirational platitude, Andrea lost his aspirations long ago. Heaven will credit me for my intentions, he thinks, and forgive me my failures. To have been capable of greatness is enough.

And so, we're asked to mark the distances between Andrea and Lucrezia, between who Andrea is and who he might have been. Browning's principal tools in marking these distances, his brush and palette knife, are metaphor and line length, tone and rhythm. His frame is the dramatic monologue, a form he more or less invented. In these monologues, we're given one speaker and a silent, or perhaps merely unheard, audience. "This, this, this face" Andrea says, looking at Lucrezia, but she says nothing, or nothing we can hear. Such is Browning's skill that her silence is as loud as his voice. It gives his words their isolated purity and gives the poem its fullness and its emptiness. Even an inspired painter couldn't paint his voice and her silence. Nor could that painter paint the distance between Andrea and the painter he might have been.

You'll have noticed that, for all his bravura technique, Browning has some trouble counting: Rafael, Agnolo, Andrea, Lucrezia, "up to God, all three," he writes. Elsewhere, Andrea imagines himself as two:

> "Had I been two, another and myself,
> Our head would have o'erlooked the world!" No doubt.

"Our head"? Is Andrea singular or plural? Thoughts of unled lives trouble the smallest particles of our language, disturbing pronouns—and not only for Andrea. Sometimes I think that most of my time writing this book has been spent changing "I" to "you" to "they" to "we" and back to "you."

"Evidently there are 2 Brownings," Henry James reported to his sister, Alice: "an esoteric & an exoteric. The former never peeps out in society, & the latter hasn't a ray of suggestion of *Men & Women*." (*Men and Women* is the title of the collection in which "Andrea del Sarto" first appeared.) How, James wondered, a little vexed, could this shrill and vulgar gossip have written such urbane

poems? And written so confoundingly many of them? In response, not to say revenge, James published "The Private Life," a
story about a man modeled on Browning. This man, Clare Vawdrey, is an author and social success, a smooth talker continually
in demand. His calendar is booked weeks in advance. People ask
how he can write so much and so well, given that he seems always
to be out about town. But then we learn his secret: Vawdrey is, in
fact, "two," another and himself. When one of him is out dining,
the other is back at his desk, composing the works that have made
him famous. Evidently, as Andrea suspected, being two has its advantages: while it isn't said that Vawdrey "o'erlooked the world,"
he is thought to be "the greatest . . . of our literary glories."

To be in the presence of meaning but not in its possession: once
this would have been an intuition of god. Andrea looks to heaven,
Vawdrey is glorified, God hangs fire, and we fly toward the sun
on waxy wings.

I've been saying that painters and poets find inspiration in our
shared singularity—our separation from each other—and in our
attempts to understand and perhaps escape it. They aren't alone
in their fascination, of course; novelists and filmmakers share it
as well. As we'll see, psychologists have built an industry out of
other lives, and philosophers have been preoccupied by them
from the start. "No one," wrote Aristotle, "would choose to have
all that is good (as for instance God is in complete possession of
the good) on condition of becoming someone else, but only on
condition of still being just himself." Aristotle's reasoning was
psychological: we don't want to give ourselves up. Much later,
Leibniz would argue the same point on logical grounds. "What

would be the use," he wrote, "of becoming the King of China on the condition that you forget what you have been? Would this not be the same thing as God creating a King of China at the same time as he destroyed you?"

It's true that no one asked Aristotle to be God, nor Leibniz to be the king of China; they're declining jobs they haven't been offered. It turns out this is something of a habit among philosophers. But I take them to be responding not to a real possibility but to a real actuality, the fact of being one person. Like the writers and painters I've been studying, they're trying to figure out what we are by figuring out what we're not. (What I'm trying to figure out is why we try to figure out what we are *in this way*.)

———

Because our thinking about these matters is so often muddy, philosophers have had to make and remake their arguments. No one, wrote the philosophical essayist William Hazlitt, ever wishes to be someone else, instead of himself; it would be "to exist by proxy." No man, "if he had his choice, would be the angel Gabriel to-morrow! What is Gabriel to him but a splendid vision?" We might want to have this or that trait belonging to someone else, this man's art or that man's scope, "but we would still be ourselves, to possess and enjoy all these." Like Aristotle, Hazlitt thinks that we have a primitive attachment to ourselves that runs beneath all our emotions, happy and unhappy. It's not vanity, exactly, but something more elemental and stubborn.

I've loved people who've made me desolate. But what Hazlitt has noticed is that I can love that desolation itself. Over time, even memories I once couldn't touch now return tenderly to me. I see the sidewalk, the slant of sunlight, the gray suit of an appalled passerby, and the hurt on my child's face. Whatever else they are, these memories are *mine*. "We would sooner be miserable after our own fashion," Hazlitt writes, in a strikingly Freudian remark, "than happy after theirs." We want not some abstract happiness, "but a happiness suited to our tastes and faculties—that has become a part of ourselves, by habit and enjoyment—that is endeared to us by a thousand recollections, privations, and sufferings." As for other people? Well, Hazlitt says, "their thoughts are not our thoughts—their happiness is not our happiness."

———

When I want to be someone else, what is it I want? It can't be that I want to be someone else entirely. That would confuse change with replacement. When—at last—I arrange my robes around the throne and receive the crown on my brow, part of me will remain to enjoy the coronation. But what part? What is it that I'm attached to when I'm attached to myself?

This is the sort of question, at once rational and absurd, that philosophers love—philosophers and comics. Ted Cohen tells a story of a man named Lev, living in Eastern Europe. One day, Lev tells a friend, "If I were the Czar, I would be richer than the Czar."

"How could that be?" asks his friend. "If you were the Czar, you would have all the Czar's wealth, and so you would be exactly as rich as the Czar. How could you be richer?"

"Well," says Lev, "if I were the Czar, on the side I would give Hebrew lessons."

———

Cohen tells this joke while making an argument that understanding others requires the imaginative movement we associate with literature. "Understanding one another involves thinking of oneself as another," he writes, and the talent for doing so "must

be related to the talent for thinking of one thing as another"—
that is, the "talent for metaphor." When I ask questions such
as these:

   What if I were Robert Pinsky?
   What if I were a Christian?
   What if I were a lover of Wagner's music?

I create metaphors such as these:

   I am Robert Pinsky.
   I am a Christian.
   I am a Wagner lover.

I put myself in another's place, Cohen says, and imagine what it's
like to be him or her. Perhaps I imagine a particular person (the
poet Robert Pinsky); perhaps a type of person (Christian, Wagner
lover). Perhaps I imagine a fictional character. In any case, I craft
a little metaphor for myself; I count one as two and two as one.

———————

Metaphors are tools used more often and unembarrassedly by
poets and novelists, of course, than by philosophers. It was in the
middle of his remarkable investigation of literary language in his
book *Seven Types of Ambiguity* that the poet and critic William
Empson found himself questioning the very value of the thing he'd
been studying. He's been thinking about the ambiguity of puns,
where two ideas are given by a single word, but he has metaphors
in mind, too. Why, he asks himself, would you "use one word with
an effort when there is time enough to say two more simply"? It's a
startling question for a poet or critic. Why do we use figurative

language? Empson's thoughts turn to a passage in Marcel Proust's *À la recherche du temps perdu* where the narrator points to our ability to remember the life we lived in one place while now living in another. Empson picks up where Proust leaves off: "In any one place (atmosphere, mental climate) life is intolerable; in any two it is an ecstasy. Is it the number two, one is forced to speculate, which is of this encouraging character? Is to live in $n+1$ places necessarily more valuable than to live in n?" Although speaking about where we live, Empson is thinking about how we talk and write. Why do we like words that are overfull of meaning? Why do some people spend their lives seeking them out? "Proust's belief," Empson writes, "is very convincing; that the pleasure in style is continually to be explained by just such a releasing and knotted duality, where those who have been wedded in the argument are bedded together in the phrase; that one must assume that $n+1$ is more valuable than n for any but the most evasively mystical theory of value."

I don't say this is the most lucid stretch of prose I've ever read, but I like it even in its obscurity. I like Empson's combination of poetic luxury and mathematic austerity. (Sometimes I've thought that I was writing a study of the number, word, and person "one.") But I also like the way that he exemplifies what he describes. To explain metaphor, he makes one: his phrasing beds what his argument has wed. I take him to be saying that when the private procreations of metaphor consecrate the daylit ceremonies of reasoned argument, the offspring both knots and releases us, binds and frees us—as language does, as children do.

———

Adam Phillips describes a session with one of his patients, a scene Dickensian in its comedy and its vulnerability, and in its faith that a child's superficial errors can express deeper truths:

An eight-year-old girl who was referred to me for school phobia—that had begun a year after her sister was born— told me in her second session that when she grew up she was "going to do clothing." I said, "Make clothes for people?" and she said, "No, no, clothing ... you know, when you make everyone wear the same uniform, like the headmistress does ... we learned about it in biology." I said, "If everyone wears the same uniform no one's special." She thought about this for a bit and then said, "Yes, no one's special but everyone's safe." I was thinking then, though I couldn't find a way of saying it, that if everyone was the same there would be no envy but she interrupted my thoughts by saying, "The teacher told us that when you do clothing you don't need a mummy and daddy, you just need a scientist, a man ... it's like twins, all the babies are the same." There was so much in all this that I couldn't choose which bit to pick up, I could only apparently carry on with the conversation. I said, "If your sister was exactly the same as you maybe you could go to school"; and she said "Yes" with some relish, "I could be at home and school at the same time ... everything!"

At home and school at the same time: in any two places, ecstasy. In her words this child has all she lacks—everything! As for Phillips, hearing what she has to say, listening for all she doesn't say, he can't keep up. He's in the presence of meaning but not in its possession, and it's exhilarating.

———

To imagine other paths down which I might have traveled is to imagine *more* life for myself: this *and* that, $n + 1$. I see another world within this one, a world I can almost touch, almost taste. It's part of this world as shadows are part of things, as memories are part of perceptions, as dreams are part of day. But a welling heart can also be a longing one. With a slight settling of my mood, my imagined life makes this one seem like less. Instead of adding to the world, my unled life subtracts from it. It was when a friend brought her daughter to me that I felt my childlessness most. The imaginary child I lacked and loved was closer to me than the one in my arms. You may say that it was only a fantasy that I lacked, but then I'd say that you underestimate how much of the life we lead *is* fantasy. What is it Billie says? "I'll be looking at the moon, but I'll be seeing you."

———

Some distinctions:

1. I want to be me but with some different features: change.
2. I want to be not me but someone else entirely: replacement.
3. I want to be me and someone else: $n+1$—or, perhaps, $n-1$.

But these desires blur into each other; sometimes it's hard to know which I feel.

———

In Randall Jarrell's poem "Next Day," a woman drives home from grocery shopping. Like Dennis's realtor, she's stalled in busy immobility, and begins to ruminate.

I am afraid, this morning, of my face.
It looks at me
From the rear-view mirror, with the eyes I hate,

The smile I hate. Its plain, lined look
Of gray discovery
Repeats to me: "You're old." That's all, I'm old.

And yet I'm afraid, as I was at the funeral
I went to yesterday.
My friend's cold made-up face, granite among its
    flowers,
Her undressed, operated-on, dressed body
Were my face and body.
As I think of her and I hear her telling me

How young I seem; I am exceptional;
I think of all I have.
But really no one is exceptional,
No one has anything, I'm anybody,
I stand beside my grave
Confused with my life, that is commonplace and
    solitary.

It's as lucid an expression of confusion as one might want. "Her
cold made-up face, granite among its flowers / Her undressed,
operated-on, dressed body / Were my face and body." The speaker
is her friend, yet her friend lies there, and she stands here. And
as I sit reading, I join them, though one is dead, the other living,
and neither real.

———

I'm anybody and exceptional, commonplace and solitary. Although I may feel singular and separate, perhaps captive and
confined, I'm also a member of many groups, with other people
in them comparable to me, leading lives comparable to mine, that

might have been mine. Perhaps the group is as small as Jarrell's pair of friends, perhaps as large as the group of all people, perhaps as large as the group of all living creatures. Probably it's somewhere in between. We're siblings or stepsiblings, classmates or colleagues, lovers of one woman, inhabitants of the same city. Perhaps we've only shared a chance moment, been present at the same opportunity, the same catastrophe, in the past. One way or another, we've been gathered together, each of us and all of us, gathered as Bruegel gathered people for his census. We are, as we ambiguously and precisely say, "one of a kind."

Early on, I said that poetry offered a heightened experience of verging on and perhaps coming to meaning; now I'm saying that it also offers a heightened experience of being with others, at once singular and commonplace. This suggests that one way (not the only way) we experience understanding is as an escape from isolation. You're reading a difficult poem and feel mentally claustrophobic; fragmentary thoughts cram your head. But when the poem begins to make sense, space opens up, light enters, and with it other people.

———

One of the fascinations of Jessie Redmon Fauset's novel *Plum Bun* is the way it evokes the doubled condition of being exceptional and anybody. The heroine of the novel, Angela, grows up in 1920s Philadelphia with her white father, her black mother, and her sister, Jinny. Fauset draws the differences between the sisters sharply: Angela is light-skinned and Jinny dark; Angela takes after their mother, Jinny after their father; Angela doesn't care for church, Jinny is devout. That they are different is immediately clear to us, but for the sisters themselves it's something they need to learn. "We've each just got to face the fact that you and I are two separate people and we've got to live our lives apart," Jinny says, "not like the Siamese twins. And each of us will have to go her chosen way." It is a remarkable thought, that we must learn that we are separate from others. And evidently, it can't be taken in all at once, for Angela must continue learning it throughout the novel: she measures her distance from others over and over, deciding who she is like and how she is like them. With whom does she belong?

While Jinny stays in Philadelphia, content to lead a placid life as a teacher, Angela moves to New York, determined to be an artist. She immediately falls in love with the city's hum and buzz; it seems endless. The wind is on her skin; everything simmers and shakes. Reading, we can feel the energy of the city become converted into exhilarated creativity. Angela rides "on the crest of a wave of excitement and satisfaction" which she thinks will "never wane, never break, never be spent." She delights in the street life of her block and delights in the people there, the young women and businessmen, the errand boys and theatergoers, the pedestrians and the poor. Looking at the street scene, she dreams of making a great painting, which she'll call "Fourteenth Street types." She will take her census, and so channel the power of the city; gathering and classifying the people around her, she rides her wave of excitement. But as she looks, it suddenly occurs to her that she, too, might be seen as a type, not unique but merely a person like any other. Her wave of excitement and satisfaction suddenly washes past her, and a vast sadness takes its place. Are there people more alive, she wonders, "more sentient to the joy, the adventure of living, even than she, to whom she would also be a 'type"? Although this wave of worry also passes, it returns throughout the novel. Is she exceptional or common?

In New York, Angela passes as white and must repeatedly decide whether she will continue to do so. These moments of decision define the plot of Fauset's novel. When Jinny comes to town, will Angela acknowledge or deny her? When Angela's lover shows himself to be racist, will she leave him? When a black student is denied a fellowship that Angela wins, will she protest? Her story is a series of turning points: Will I continue to pass? she asks. What would happen if people knew I'm black? What would my life be like?

———

"If I were a man, I could be President," Angela remarks. It's a common sort of speculation, to imagine yourself having been born a different sex or race, though more common for some than for others. Fauset's career has invited critics to speculate in exactly this way about her. Had she "not been a 'colored woman,'" writes David Levering Lewis, Fauset "might have sought work with a New York publishing house. . . . There is no telling what she would have done had she been a man, given her first-rate mind and formidable efficiency at any task." Angela and Levering are speculating not about having made different choices along a path, or having had different luck, but about having had a different path altogether—about having been dealt a different hand. Regret is a luxury given to those born to choice and chance.

It isn't an absolute distinction: Angela can pass as white, after all, and though she evidently can't pass as a man, others could. But some alternatives are more easily imagined than others, the difference a matter of the person and the culture. "We know perfectly well that a great deal of what we are, in terms of memory, character, and bodily development, is the product of accidental factors which we can readily conceive to have been otherwise," writes Bernard Williams.

> "If my parents had, as they considered doing, emigrated when I was two . . ."—yet it would still have been me. Suppose, further, that I had had different parents, who had borne me in a different year, a different century even. . . . Such speculations can retain a grip on the imagination only up to a certain point.

Where these speculations lose their grip is a revealing fact about a person and about the configurations of identity in their society. But it's also a revealing fact about the genres we use to make those speculations. With her ready opportunities for thoughtful reflection, Angela offers promising material for a novelist, who can craft for her a deep character and dramatic plot. *Plum Bun* is about her, not her sister; a life like Jinny's, with fewer choices and chances, wouldn't have provided Fauset with the material she needed. About Jinny, evidently, "there's no telling what she might have done."

Reading stories is one way we explore attitudes of attachment to ourselves. Angela is first delighted with herself and then despairing as she looks over the people on her block. There are other attitudes one can adopt, of course. One can be amused with oneself, or earnest, reckless, experimental, smug, interested, judgmental, intermittently bored . . . . Fiction provides a wild taxonomy of such attitudes. More than that, it studies what it is to be committed to yourself at all. It makes of our commitment to continue reading an allegory for our commitment to continue being ourselves.

In Thomas Hardy's *Far from the Madding Crowd,* the young, flashy Sergeant Troy pauses to compare his life with those of others who "may actually resemble him in every particular":

> Troy had felt, in his transient way, hundreds of times, that he could not envy other people their condition, because the possession of that condition would have necessitated a different personality, when he desired no other than his own. He had not minded the peculiarities of his birth, the vicissitudes of his life, the meteor-like uncertainty of all that related to him, because these appertained to the hero of his story, without whom there would have been no story at all for him.

Troy's commitment to being himself, happy or unhappy, is a commitment to being the hero of a story, his story. Even Troy's uncertainty matters to him. His need to be in a story comes *before* his desire for happiness—it's what makes his life meaningful.

———

If painting studies our separation with line, color, and form; and poetry studies it with metaphor, tone, line length, and large-scale structure; and philosophy studies it with reasoned argumentation; how does fiction study it? To begin an answer, let me cite one last philosopher dreaming of glory. "Suppose I conceive it to be possible that I might have been Napoleon," writes Williams,

> and mean by this that there might have been a world which contained a Napoleon exactly the same as the Napoleon

that our world contained, except that he would have been me. What could be the difference between the actual Napoleon and the imagined one? . . . If the activity of imagining being Napoleon involved in any important way imagery, it is bound, I think, to involve participation imagery. Images of myself being Napoleon can scarcely merely be images of the physical figure of Napoleon, for they will not in themselves have enough of me in them— an external view would lose the essence of what makes such imagining so much more compelling about myself than they are about another. They will rather be images of, for instance, the desolation at Austerlitz as viewed by me vaguely aware of my short stature and my cockaded hat, my hand in my tunic.

It's a self-congratulatory fantasy, imagining yourself as the emperor—"testosterone-y," as a friend put it. But the picture of participation seems about right, a good description of what can happen when I think of changing my state with that of someone else—king, god, czar, mogul, president, mayor, head of the local motor vehicles bureau, anyone. And it also seems a good description of what it would be like to read a story about the bloody fields of Belgium, told from Napoleon's perspective. "Participation imagery" is a fair phrase for what fiction offers. In writing novels, and in reading them, we can see something of what it would be to be one traveler on two roads.

———

To participate is to take part; but it's to take *only* part. I'm not wholly at Austerlitz, not cockaded, certainly not short. I put myself in Napoleon's place yet remain myself. To say it that way makes participating seem deliberate, but as I read it happens un-consciously and quickly. When Emma is rude to Miss Bates, I don't *try* to feel shame; I feel it before I know it. Another word for this participation is sympathy, long seen to be a defining moral and aesthetic virtue of fiction. "Art is the nearest thing to life," as George Eliot put it—not life itself, but nearest to it. "It is a mode of amplifying experience and extending our contact with our fellow-men beyond the bounds of our personal lot." Eliot's long novels show how laborious and important she believed such imaginative travel could be in life, and how necessary, then, the training of art. "The greatest benefit we owe to the artist," she wrote, "whether painter, poet or novelist, is the extension of our sympathies."

When I read Austen's *Persuasion,* my sympathetic participation is solicited right away: I open the book and read about a man opening a book.

> Sir Walter Elliot, of Kellynch Hall, in Somersetshire, was a man who, for his own amusement, never took up any book but the Baronetage; there he found occupation for an idle hour, and consolation in a distressed one; there . . . he could read his own history with an interest which never failed—this was the page at which the favorite volume always opened: "ELLIOT OF KELLYNCH HALL."

It's Austen at her most analytical and impish. Here's a man I can't help but resemble if I'm to continue: like him, I'm a reader. We're members of the same group. But he's vain and empty-headed; when he reads, he looks for himself. I have no desire to belong to a group that includes him in it. And so, Austen invites me in and warns me off at the same time; she includes me in her story even as she makes me wary of being included. Enter if you like, she says, but watch the company you keep. The remainder of *Persuasion* will repeat the invitation and repeat the caution. We're led to ask ourselves, how are we like these characters and how not? What counts as participation and what as exclusion? We're absorbed and distanced at once: it's the dance that defines readers' attention.

Eight years ago, Sir Walter's daughter Anne followed the advice of her surrogate mother, Lady Russell, and broke an engagement with the young and promising but poor Captain Wentworth. "A few months had seen the beginning and the end of their acquaintance; but, not with a few months ended Anne's share of suffering from it. Her attachment and regrets had, for a long time, clouded every enjoyment of youth; and an early loss of bloom and spirits had been their lasting effect." Wentworth left for the sea and for war, marooning Anne among her family, a vain and ignorant tribe. With them she's singular, "only Anne," and, as Lady Russell remarks, "it is singularity which often makes the worst part of our suffering." In her solitude, Anne has ample opportunity for reflection about what might have been. The conclusion of those reflections is to be persuaded that she would "have been a happier woman in maintaining the engagement, than she had been in the sacrifice of it." But she didn't maintain the engagement, and that made all the difference: "Once so much to each other! Now nothing!"

Austen sketches all of this quickly; it's prelude to her plot. The novel really begins when Wentworth reappears. He's everything Anne hoped he would be: charming, successful, and wealthy. But he'll have little to do with her. He courts other women while she looks on, and we look on with her. We see the world through her eyes, from her elevated position. But like us, she's alone and out of the action. While Wentworth dances with the women of the neighborhood, Anne plays the piano. Her music sets the characters in motion; she watches them come together and move apart, but she doesn't dance. As she looks on, she tries hard to cultivate a rational acceptance of her solitude.

Anne and Wentworth are reunited at novel's end, of course. But Austen makes clear how lucky they've been: had Sir Walter not needed to lease out his home; had he not leased it to Captain Wentworth's sister; had Wentworth not been free to visit that sister; had neighboring women not been so alluringly unmarried as to encourage him to extend that visit; had there not been opportunities for Anne to distinguish herself from the crowd; had the men not taken an inexperienced hunting dog out; had that low rambling bush not been just there when they all went for a walk; had that passing stranger on the Cobb not been so open in his admiration of Anne. . . . Austen's plot is a chain of contingencies that occur during the brief period between Napoleon's exile to and escape from Elba—that is, during the few months when an English sailor, lucky enough to have survived war's dangers, might be on shore and have the opportunity to make love to a woman. Although we know from the beginning where we're going, we come to know that Anne and Wentworth are lucky. *Persuasion* is a novel of happenstance inevitability, like any other.

When, at last, Wentworth embraces Anne, we're told that in their conversation the couple "returned again into the past, more exquisitely happy, perhaps, in their reunion, than when it had first been projected." They walked through the hills of Bath and "there, as they slowly paced the gradual ascent, heedless of every group around them, seeing neither sauntering politicians, bustling house-keepers, flirting girls, nor nursery-maids and children, they could indulge in those retrospections and acknowledgements . . . which were so poignant and so ceaseless in interest." Their conversation, we're told, "would make the present hour a blessing indeed; and prepare for it all the immortality which the happiest recollections of their own future lives could bestow." Among others but separate from them, Anne and Wentworth become narrator and audience of their lives, linking past and present and future to preserve time from time's decay. Love's first impulse is to tell its story, and so make an everyday eternity. "All the little variations of the last week were gone through," we're told, "and of yesterday and to-day there could scarcely be an end."

It is, I think, the loveliest sentence in nineteenth-century English fiction. And yet, even in their gentle exhilaration, the lovers can't help but imagine what hasn't happened. "Tell me," Wentworth asks,

> "if, when I returned to England in the year eight, with a few thousand pounds, and was posted into the Laconia, if I had then written to you, would you have answered my letter? Would you, in short, have renewed the engagement then?"
> "Would I!" was all her answer; but the accent was decisive enough.

It's a Wonderful Life

If "The Road Not Taken" is the classic poem of unled lives, and "The Jolly Corner" the classic story, then Frank Capra's *It's a Wonderful Life* is the classic film. As the movie opens, or just after, we're shown the movie of a man's life, screened for us and for an angel named Clarence (Henry Travers) by his angelic superiors. The man, George Bailey (Jimmy Stewart), means to kill himself, and Clarence has been assigned to save him; the movie we see is meant to brief Clarence on his assignment. With him, we learn about George's lifelong attempt to escape the small town of Bedford Falls, his sense of being under-employed by life, his blurry love of his wife, Mary, his tireless rectitude and growing despair. Now it's Christmas Eve and George is at his wit's end. Believing that the world would have been better had he never been born, he stands on a bridge, determined to throw himself into the wintery water below.

In order to save him, Clarence descends to the bridge and teaches George as he himself has just been taught: he shows him a film—the film we have just seen, in fact, but without its hero. George's gets what he wants: we see the world as it would have been without him. It's as if Capra were to accept the old charge that movies are merely exercises in wish-fulfillment, but then to point out that we often don't know what our wishes are. Clarence uses a film to show George what he truly wants, and so save him. Together they wander through Bedford Falls as it would have been, unknown and unable to help those George loves. Absorbed in what he watches, but powerless, he discovers his desire to live.

On the face of it, Capra's film may seem an exception to much of what I've been saying. George Bailey doesn't merely wish to have taken a different path; he wishes to have had no path at all. More than that, the gods of this film are neither ignorant nor impotent: not only do they know the lives people have lived and the lives they haven't, but they can do something about those lives. But I've been saying that thoughts of unled lives tend towards the extreme, towards all or nothing, and that they often represent the extreme in mild tones. In wishing never to have lived, mild George is certainly being extreme. And, although Clarence is an angel, he's a very human one—distracted, flustered, self-doubting. He works in what seems to be a very human bureaucracy, a place more like an invisible Dickensian counting house than a heaven. He's an "Angel Second Class," eager for promotion. (I picture a spinster sister tending house for him.) And he comes to us as a friend. Indeed, he's a friend to whom one can write letters, in the form of prayers, and from whom, more surprisingly, one can receive letters. The movie ends when George reads Clarence's note, inscribed his river-wrinkled copy of *Tom Sawyer*: "Dear George: Remember no man is a failure who has friends. P.S. Thanks for the wings! Love, Clarence."

The lines of connection extend further than this. George is trapped in Bedford Falls and desperate to leave. He's held in place by his young family, by his career as a banker, by the respect others have for him, and by bad luck. Most of all, he is held in place by his own upright character. He's as true as an anchor line when the anchor has caught. When the hateful, small-town tyrant Mr. Potter (Lionel Barrymore) tells him as much, George doesn't deny it. "George Bailey is not a common, ordinary yokel," Potter says.

> He's an intelligent, smart, ambitious young man who hates
> his job, who hates the building and loan, almost as much

as I do. A young man who's been dying to get out on his own ever since he was born. A young man . . . the smartest one of the crowd, mind you, a young man who has to sit by and watch his friends go places, because he's trapped. Yes, sir, trapped into frittering his life away. . . . Do I paint a correct picture, or do I exaggerate?

George is a singular everyman in this unremarkable town, like other young men but set apart. He's not just smarter, but slightly older, more mature, taller. We measure his distance from those around him. George's brother, Harry, leaves Bedford Falls for noble wartime service, heroism, and fame. The film calls this "meeting the president." His friend Sam leaves Bedford Falls for a tinsel paradise of wealth, booze, and flirtation. The film calls this "New York." They travel and George stays at home.

To sit by and watch friends go places: a parable of envy. I could be there, and should be there, but I'm here. I feel intensely apart, but also intensely connected. For in saying I belong in another's place, I silently claim a likeness with them: how else could I fill their space? Or, rather, since my likeness seems already to have been established, I don't claim it but discover it. When Aristotle began listing kinds of envious people, it was hard for him to stop: the ambitious, the small-minded, those who care about reputation, honor, fortune, success, wisdom, those who want something they ought to have or have had, those who have fallen just a little short of something they desire, those who don't have something they want, those who have spent too much on something, those in high places, old men. . . . But he did at last come to a conclusion about his list: "We envy those who are near us in time, place, age, or reputation," he says. We envy our kind. "Hence the line: Ay, kin can even be jealous of their kin. . . . Hence the saying:

potter against potter." Envy is like sympathy in this way; it bespeaks similarity to others—maybe many others, maybe only one other. But while sympathy can seem hard work—I struggle to put myself in the place of another person—envy is effortless. I already am in that person's place, or should be. It's my place by right or desert or natural gift. The problem is that somehow I'm not there.

And so, George is defined against the friends he tries not to envy. But he is also defined against an older generation of men who have stayed in Bedford Falls. He has inherited his father's intelligence and decency along with his uneven defenses against resignation and his reserves of masculine affection. When his father died, George stepped into his place at the building and loan. His similarity to his father, and his rightness for the position at the building and loan is marked by comparison with his Uncle Billy (Thomas Mitchell), whom one might think would have taken over. Billy is a widower, like George's father, but he has been undone—presumably by his wife's death—and blunders through the movie in ramshackle and kindly distraction. It's a sign of Capra's redemptive impulse, as my student Sarah Ross pointed out to me, that Clarence is a redeemed Billy, an image of what Billy will be as a star. In heaven, the good-hearted find their intentions effective. But Billy is no man of business.

And, finally, George is like Potter—like Potter and against Potter, and Potter knows it. They're both bankers whose loans enable others to build houses. They are (apart from George's wife, Mary) the two smartest people in the town. And they're both paralyzed. There's an open suggestion that Potter's wheelchair is a movie director's chair, the chair of someone who administers the world's every detail but cannot act within it. He has power at the expense of experience. He controls Bedford Falls but doesn't truly live in it, and he envies those who do. With similar powers, George worries that he has succumbed to a similar fate. Bailey Park, the subdivision he builds, looks like nothing so much as a movie set.

It's Potter's psychological acuity, then, as well as his business cunning, that leads him to offer George a job at his bank, more or less inviting George to take his place. Potter's offer gives Stewart a chance to show off his signature slow-dawning indignation: he's too innocent to see Potter's perfidy at first, and too smart not to see it a moment later. When George returns from their meeting to Mary, lying in their darkened bedroom, Potter's voice lingers in his head, darkness audible. We hear it in a voice-over, a sonic afterimage. (One moment is superimposed on another; we're given two scenes as one.) "You wouldn't mind living in the nicest house in town. Buying your wife a lot of fine clothes, going to New York on a business trip a couple of times a year. Maybe to Europe once in a while." Potter's words echo a speech George made earlier, when he was courting Mary, and we now hear that speech again as Potter's voice resolves into George's:

> I know what I'm going to do tomorrow and the next day and next year and the year after that. I'm shaking the dust of this crummy little town off my feet, and I'm going to see the world. . . . And I'm going to build things. I'm going to build airfields. I'm going to build skyscrapers a hundred stories high. I'm going to build a bridge a mile long.

Potter seems to voice George's own desires back to him. But then, as he sleepwalks through his thoughts, George notices a sketch Mary made long ago of him lassoing the moon. George's voice-over continues, still in the tones of his youth: "What is it you want,

Mary? You want the moon? If you do, just say the word; I'll throw
a lasso around it and pull it down for you." Potter has voiced
George's dreams for him and proposed to make them come true,
just as George, when a young man with the world all before him,
voiced Mary's dreams for her and proposed to make them come
true. But they're poor now, and George has just turned down an
opportunity to make them rich. Has he been a false tempter, then,
like Potter?

The answer comes obliquely. As we watch George drift through
the dark bedroom, we hear Mary's voice start to sing the couple's
theme song, "Buffalo Gals": "Buffalo gals, won't you come out tonight / Come out tonight, come out tonight / Buffalo gals, won't
you come out tonight / And we'll dance by the light of the moon."
George has silently asked her to say the word, and she does, as if
she heard his thoughts. It's initially unclear whether George is remembering Mary's voice or hearing it—whether her song is only
inside his head or also outside it. In truth, it doesn't really matter.
Potter might know George, but Mary is part of him: they dream
together, neither solely singular. When George looks in the
bedroom mirror, it's his wife we see, and when he does talk to
her, there in the dark, he learns she's pregnant. And so we've
returned to the difficulties in counting Mary, the mystery of
being one and two.

That Capra studies what it is to be neither one nor two but
none is evident enough: we're first given George Bailey, and then
he's subtracted from the movie. He learns what it is to be no-
body. More than that, even when he does live in Bedford Falls,
George is only partially present to his world. When his father
has a stroke, when there's a run on the bank, when he falls in
love, he snaps to attention; otherwise, his thoughts loiter elsewhere,

inward. (George is related to Uncle Billy, after all.) In this, Capra exploits Stewart's capacity for charismatic withdrawal, his ability to be visibly absent. When Clarence later shows us the world without George in it, he merely makes more noticeable what has been true from the start: George has never truly lived in Bedford Falls. He left town long ago; the task of the movie is to arrange for his return.

And yet, whenever George Bailey does appear, Jimmy Stewart appears. We're given two people at once. Here's a moment when talking about our unlived lives courts fatuity. Surely it's a bit much to talk about something like "the ecstatic doubleness of acting." No doubt I could find a better phrase. But I'm encouraged by the fact that such doubleness has preoccupied filmmakers themselves. Consider the number of films that depend on a character's sense of being misrecognized, taken as someone else, living the life of someone else, even while remaining him or herself. *North by Northwest* is maybe the most famous example. Continually taken to be George Kaplan, Roger O. Thornhill continually insists that he is not. As Stanley Cavell points out, the Hitchcockian irony is that George Kaplan doesn't exist; he is no one, invented by the CIA as a dummy figure in a cat and mouse game played by the Agency and the coolly villainous Philip Vandamm (James Mason). This is to say that Roger Thornhill is himself or no one— he is mistaken for no one. But at the same time, Roger Thornhill is always Cary Grant (who also, in a different sense, can be mistaken for no one). There's hardly a scene, as Cavell notes, in which someone doesn't accuse Thornhill of being an actor or charge him with being a bad one. It's as if Hitchcock were to say that, while being no one comes readily enough, being exactly and happily one person is an achievement.

The most beautiful philosophical description of this achievement that I know comes in *The Gay Science,* where Nietzsche imagines us coming one night to a fork in our road, presided over by yet another divinity, this one not impotent but with a decisive power. What if, Nietzsche says,

> a demon were to steal after you into your loneliest loneliness and say to you: "This life as you now live it and have lived it, you will have to live once more and innumerable times more; and there will be nothing new in it, but every pain and every joy and every thought and sigh and everything unutterably small or great in your life will have to return to you, all in the same succession and sequence—even this spider and this moonlight between the trees, and even this moment and I myself. The eternal hourglass of existence is turned upside down again and again, and you with it, speck of dust!"
>
> Would you not throw yourself down and gnash your teeth and curse the demon who spoke thus? Or have you once experienced a tremendous moment when you would have answered him: "You are a god and never have I heard anything more divine."

Neither a new life after this one, nor a different life now: this one life, only, again and then again, always the same, even down to the spider and the moonlight between the trees.

If being no one is a threat, and being one person an achievement, being two people (and one of them Cary Grant) can seem to be a dream. Movie stars exhilarate because they give apparently effortless expression to the human capacities we share with them. They have discovered our capacities and so discovered us. They realize, Cavell writes, "that we can still be found, behind our disguises of bravado and cowardice, by someone, perhaps a god, capable of defeating our self-defeats." But stars also exhilarate because they transcend our capacities. In being two people, they escape from singularity. While Clarence's film presents a world from which George Bailey has been subtracted, Capra's film presents a world to which Jimmy Stewart has been added. (A world in which *he* goes unrecognized—in which even his mother doesn't know him—is a bad world indeed.) As the art historian Erwin Panofsky remarked long ago, "the character in film . . . lives and dies with the actor."

And so, *It's a Wonderful Life* casually studies the first essential feature of our stories, the idea of singularity, a life in solitary confinement dreaming of escape, and finding that escape in becoming two—two in marriage, two in pregnancy, two in business, two in acting. Capra's movie also introduces the second essential feature of our stories, the forked road. I've already noticed that traveling is a central motif in the movie and provides a familiar emblem for the shape of life as a journey, in this case one with bridges, crossroads, and railroads; with travel brochures, advertisements, and a very large, unused suitcase; with long shots of Jimmy Stewart loping along the streets. But Capra transforms this cliché. He thinks through its possibilities and shows us something new.

Early in the film, Harry falls into an icy pond and George calls to the other boys: "Make a chain! A chain!" Lying flat on the ground, each boy holds the feet of the boy in front of him, and together they reach into the water to rescue the drowning boy. It's an image of the community the movie will celebrate, a community directed by one man, to a purpose. It's also an image for the plot of that movie—not a road but a chain, forged by its awkwardly commanding hero. Capra took this image of plot as a chain from Dickens. When the ghost of Jacob Marley appears at the start of *A Christmas Carol,* he's garlanded with a chain that he made link by link: "I girded it on of my own free will," he says, "and of my own free will I wore it." Marley then ushers Scrooge to what is effectively a movie of the miser's life, a linked series of scenes. But Capra's episodic, enchained film also echoes Dickens's *Great Expectations,* a story told by the stepson of a blacksmith, who grew up by a forge and was adopted by a manacled convict who at novel's end is rescued from a river. At one point, looking back on a decisive moment in his life and plot, Dickens's narrator, Pip, speaks directly to us:

> That was a memorable day to me, for it made great changes in me. But, it is the same with any life. Imagine one selected day struck out of it, and think how different its course would have been. Pause you who read this, and think for a moment of the long chain of iron or gold, of thorns or flowers, that would never have bound you, but for the formation of the first link on one memorable day.

Pip's logic can't be pushed too far. (What happened before that memorable day? Aren't *all* days equally linked? Why *days?* Why *memorable* days?) But it's clear that Pip understands himself to be bound by the chain that is his life; and clear, too, that there were other chains that could have been forged. Forged for Pip and forged for us, forged for all of us and forged for each of us; as the critic Garrett Stewart has pointed out, because the first- and second-person plural are indistinguishable in English, Pip's address can be read as, "Pause (each of you)" and as "Pause (all of you)." Pip hails us as individuals even as he hails us as members of a group, readers of this novel. Our nature is doubled, and Pip here, with extraordinary compression, addresses that doubled nature, exceptional and anybody. So, too, does Capra, when he gives us his one extraordinary everyman, Stewart and Bailey.

The movie shown to Clarence and to us is incomplete. We don't see *everything* that happens to George Bailey; like Capra, the angels have made selections and edited out alternatives. But what we do see is a linked sequence of chance happenings that bind George, as Pip is bound: his father has a stroke, which keeps George from going to college; his brother Harry marries and moves elsewhere, leaving George in charge of the building and loan; a bank run happens to occur just as he and Mary are leaving town for their honeymoon. This chain binds his life and *is* his life. When Clarence then shows George and us the world as it would have been without him, this is what we see: had George not lived, he would not have kept the pharmacist Mr. Gower from poisoning his customers; had George not opposed him, Potter would have made the town over into a lipstick smear of nightclubs and speakeasies; had George not helped his friend Violet, she would have become a prostitute. And, had George not been alive to love her, Mary—it seems the worst of all possible horrors—would have put her hair up and become a librarian.

When Clarence comes to George at the river, we see reprised the childhood scene at the pond, when George saved his brother. With an effective if unlikely cunning, George's loving angel plunges into the icy water, knowing that George will rescue him and so allow himself to be rescued. In doing this Clarence seems to be acting on his own, but he has been summoned by the chained prayers of all the people in Bedford Falls whom George has helped. We hear them at the start of the movie, one voice after another, rising to the ears of angels. The bodies that we think of as separate are linked; the voices of different people are looped together.

This is one tidy moral of the story: the chains that bind also save. What this flustered, nightgown-clad angel standing in the moonlight among the trees has given George Bailey is the mixed gift of affirming those chains, embracing his restraints, now.

———

And so *It's a Wonderful Life,* like "The God Who Loves You," ends by encouraging a man—another realtor, of sorts—to give up thoughts of other lives and to make a home in his own. Like Carl Dennis, Capra entertains alternatives, allows us to enjoy them, and then tells us to leave them behind. We're urged to embrace the actual. George's task is not to become good, as Scrooge must become good, but to accept that he is already good. It's a lesser demand, if a more interesting one. And it's expressed not only by George's plot but also by the tone of the movie as a whole, which seems to easily accept its own goodness.

I hope I don't begrudge talent its ease, but Capra, like Dennis, seems to be playing well within his game. Compare, for instance, Browning's "Andrea Del Sarto," another conversational work of achieved facility. "I regret little," Andrea tells us, "I would change still less./Since there my past life lies, why alter it?" Here's a man who has embraced the actual. But we're not meant to celebrate him, or to imitate him. Browning's verse mimics the painter's laxness in order criticize it. The form of the poem, the very silence surrounding the painter, sets him at a distance from us. I don't doubt that Dennis and Capra worked hard and left drafts in the wastebasket, film on the floor. But they both project casual comfort with what they've done. How should I think about this? Is it the triumph of complacency or an expression of grace? By what art can art reconcile us to its limits? Of course, I also mean to ask, by what art can art can reconcile us to our limits, me to mine?

Plots

Standing in my kitchen, taking a break from editing these pages, making lunch, I listen to the radio show *This American Life.*

A Bosnian child named Emir Kamenica was living with his family in Sarajevo in the 1990s when the war started, and they fled. In telling the story of their flight, Emir emphasizes his luck: he and his sister and his mother were lucky to get a ride out of town, lucky to join a refugee convoy, lucky that the weather was warm. Even though he acknowledges that tragic things happened—his father was killed before they fled—Emir sees the story of his life as a very lucky one.

Most lucky of all, perhaps, his family was allowed to migrate to the United States, where they were taken in by an older Bosnian couple living in Atlanta. But life in Atlanta wasn't easy. Kids threatened Emir because they thought of him as white, one of maybe twenty white kids in a school of nine hundred. And his English wasn't good. He says that, when told to write an essay, he plagiarized and translated a passage from a book he had brought with him from Bosnia. "I remember I closed my essay with this bit of internal monologue, which roughly says, I'm slowly becoming a repository for decomposing sorrows, regrets, ignored injustice, and forgotten promises. I can still feel its stench. But when I get accustomed to it, I will call it experience." His teacher, Ms. Ames, was impressed. The next day, passing the essays back, she whispered in his ear, "You have to get out of this school." When she had an interview to teach at a local private school, she took him along; she didn't get the job, but he was admitted.

The rest of Emir's story moves quickly. He felt safe at the new school, could pay attention in class, did well, graduated, was given a scholarship to Harvard, received his BA, then his PhD, met his wife, was hired by the University of Chicago as a professor of economics, was immediately successful, and was granted tenure early. As Michael Lewis, who is recounting the story, remarks, "all because Ms. Ames read his plagiarized essay and was fooled by it." She was, Emir says, an angel who appeared to him and changed the course of his life.

> In everyone's life there are many forks. This is by far the biggest one. This is what made the most difference. There's no doubt that my life got onto a very different kind of a track. And I'm pretty sure that if it hadn't been for her, I would've stayed in Clarkston High School. I wouldn't have thought to apply to a private school. I most certainly wouldn't have gone to Harvard.

"It's always hard to say how your life would have turned out differently if something hadn't happened to you," Lewis says.

> But in Emir's case, there's at least one useful reference point—his Bosnian friend, Emil. Emil hadn't been airlifted out of Clarkston into some fancy private school. Instead, he had dropped out of Clarkston, done some bad things, and actually spent some time in jail. Eventually he went back to Bosnia. No Ms. Ames. No rescue.

Lewis tracks down Ms. Ames. She remembers Emir well, but remembers his story differently: Clarkston was a pretty good school, there were many white kids there, the atmosphere wasn't threatening, she had her eye on Emir for months, she has no memory of his plagiarized essay, she got the idea of helping him transfer one day when he taught the class how to diagram sentences, his math and science teachers told her that he was working at a level beyond anything they could teach him, she negotiated at length with the private school to arrange his transfer. She also says that she doesn't think any of this mattered: Emir was so hugely talented that he would have succeeded even if he had stayed in the public school. Why, then, did she pay him such close attention? Well, she muses, she and her husband had decided not to have children; perhaps her regret about that made her more eager to help him.

So, the encounter with Ms. Ames was not a decisive event—or not for Emir. But Ms. Ames tells us that once she arranged for Emir, Clarkston's best student, to be moved, the school administration cast her out of what she calls her "paradise" and transferred her to another school. Her new principal drove her so hard that she quit. Now she lives in West Virginia and works as an interior decorator. If it had not been for Emir. . . . Ms. Ames doesn't tell this story readily, but it's the story she leaves us with.

Ms. Ames's version of his story bothers Emir. But when asked, he says that he'll continue to tell his own version. He might include the fact that Ms. Ames was punished for helping him, but other than that he'll keep it as it was. Here's how Lewis closes the show:

> These stories we tell about ourselves—they're almost like our infrastructure, like railroads or highways. We can build them almost any way we want to. But once they're in place, this whole inner landscape grows up around them. So maybe the point here is that you should be careful about how you tell your story, or at least conscious of it. Because once you've told it, once you've built the highway,

it's just very hard to move it. Even if your story is about an
angel who came out of nowhere and saved your life, even
then, not even the angel herself can change it.

Roads taken and untaken, forking moments, the stories we tell
about travel and education and careers and parenting, an uncertainty about what has been true, an incapable angel, all the difference. . . . Sitting with my lunch now made, it seems to me that
these stories are everywhere, inescapable.

————

In 1982 the psychologists Daniel Kahneman and Amos Tversky
published a paper on the ways we imagine alternate pasts for ourselves. Their study recorded people's responses to everyday stories much simpler than Emir's, stories with plots stripped to their
basic elements. By now, those elements will be familiar: a fork in
the past from which roads diverged. "Mr. Crane and Mr. Tees
were scheduled to leave the airport on different flights, at the same
time. They traveled from town in the same limousine, were caught
in a traffic jam, and arrived at the airport 30 minutes after the
scheduled departure time of their flights." So far, their stories are
identical, and we can easily imagine that each man would look
back and mentally "undo" the traffic jam, as Kahneman and
Tversky put it, so that he could catch his plane. But when they
arrive at the airport, "Mr. Crane is told that his flight left on time.
Mr. Tees is told that his flight was delayed and just left five minutes ago." Who is more upset? Kahneman and Tversky had a genius for crafting stories like this one, stories that generate superficially unremarkable responses. Ninety-six percent of respondents
thought Mr. Tees would be more upset. But, then again, shouldn't
the men be equally miserable? Once they hit the traffic jam,

neither thought he would catch his plane, and neither did. Now they sit side by side in the airport, in the same position. But—of course—Mr. Tees feels worse: he can't help but think that he could have caught the plane.

In the years after Kahneman and Tversky published their paper, devising stories like this one became something of an academic industry—symptoms as much as studies of our fascination with unled lives. One paper reported that runners who finish a close second in a race will feel worse than those who finish third, if medals are given only to the first three finishers: third place finishers are relieved not to have finished a medal-less fourth, while second place finishers still dream of gold. In another study, two women are asked to flip a coin and are told that if the coin comes up the same, they'll each receive $1,000. Lisa tosses a head, then Jenny tosses a tail. Neither wins. Most people, if then asked to complete a sentence that begins "If only . . . ," will respond, "If only Jenny had tossed a head." But why not say, "If only Lisa had tossed a tail"? The women would have won the money in either case. Evidently, given a sequence like this one, we typically imagine changes in later events rather than earlier ones. Still other studies have shown that we're more likely to second-guess actions than failures to act, more likely to mentally undo features that were in our control than features that were not, more likely to change exceptional events than routine ones, and more likely to change actions that we think are inappropriate than those that we think are appropriate. On his way home from work, Stephen is delayed by several events: he, too, gets stuck in a traffic jam, then must take a detour because of a fallen log on the road, and decides to stop by his mistress's apartment. He arrives home to discover that his wife has just had a heart attack and died. He had not been there to take her to the hospital. If only. . . .

As he sits at the gate, Mr. Crane could imagine that a new air-line company had just formed, one that reserved seats for pas-sengers named Crane; and that this Crane-friendly airline had a flight leaving in ten minutes with one seat (business class) still available. But he doesn't. We don't imagine just *any* alternatives to past events. "There is an Alice-in-Wonderland quality to such examples, with their odd mixture of fantasy and reality," write Kahneman and Tversky. "If Mr. Crane is capable of imagining unicorns—and we expect he is—why does he find it relatively dif-ficult to imagine himself avoiding a 30-minute delay?" While we might be able to create any alternative pasts for ourselves, typi-cally we don't. As Kahneman and Dale Miller would later put it, "the generation of alternatives to reality appears to be quite disciplined."

In their experiments, psychologists anatomize these alterna-tives; they dissect them and label their parts. It's true that they can be reductive in their ideas of human motivation and crude in their aims: "Counterfactuals are for betterment," proclaims a book titled *If Only: How to Turn Regret into Opportunity*. But at their best, they reveal the logic beneath our irrationality. As Emir's tale shows, however, the stories that most matter to us are usu-ally less spare, less certain, and harder to quantify than those told by the psychologists. Was plagiarizing the essay really the most important forking moment in Emir's life? More important than the death of his father, so quickly passed over, or the escape from Sarajevo? More important than coming to the United States? And even if it were the most important moment, was it one event or a chain of events (fleeing Sarajevo, joining the refugee convoy, coming to the United States, finding housing, being in Ms. Ames's class, being admitted to the private school . . .)? It's even unclear who the protagonist is: we think it's Emir, but maybe it's Ms. Ames. Such stories matter most to us, this is to say, when they have the ambiguity and resonance of literature. Maybe I can put it this way: the stories devised and dissected by psychologists teach me things; the stories that matter most to me teach me nothing. At least, that's not why I read them. They make meaning for me, with me. It's a process that takes place at a different rate, with a different rhythm. I linger and return, seeking again that state of spirit in which I'm in the presence of meaning but not in its possession, where I might find out what matters and how it matters, find it once or find it again.

———

Midway through telling the story of his life, David Copperfield pauses for a bit of psychological self-analysis. The current of his feelings is tidal and brackish, agitated by incomprehension and need. For years he's felt an obscure melancholy. Now it's deepened:

> It was as undefined as ever, and addressed me like a strain of sorrowful music faintly heard in the night. I loved my wife dearly, and I was happy; but the happiness I had vaguely anticipated, once, was not the happiness I enjoyed, and there was always something missing.

> In fulfillment of the compact I have made with myself, to reflect my mind on this paper, I again examine it, closely, and bring its secrets to the light. What I missed, I still regarded—I always regarded—as something that had been a dream of my youthful fancy; that was incapable of realization; that I was now discovering to be so, with some natural pain, as all men did. But, that it would have been better for me if my wife could have helped me more, and shared the many thoughts in which I had no partner; and that this might have been; I knew.

In his solitude David makes his own company and tries to learn his own secrets. Unable to share his thoughts with Dora, he tries to share them with himself, and so with us. But his awkward syntax and punctuation—notice the semicolon thrust just before "I knew"—suggest that he can't easily cast himself in words. Language is broken, and David's questions lay bare its brokenness. What can you reasonably expect from life? How trustworthy are the expectations you formed when young? Could those expectations have been satisfied had you taken another path—had you married differently, for instance? How can you know?

In thinking back on his life, David has entered two overlapping areas of unhappy uncertainty. Is this experience of disappointed solitude common to all husbands, he wonders, or is it his alone? And would he be unhappy even if he had married someone other than Dora? For all his earnest introspection, David doesn't know. He doesn't know whether he is anybody or exceptional. He doesn't know whether his marriage was truly a fork in his road. He doesn't know what is important: "Between these two irreconcilable conclusions: the one, that what I felt was general and unavoidable; the other, that it was particular to me, and might have been different: I balanced curiously, with no distinct sense of their opposition to each other." When David thinks his feelings are particular to him, he feels separate from others, and (though he can't say it) he wishes he were more like them—that is, happily married. When he thinks his feelings are general, he thinks that all married men are lonely, and that nothing he could have done would have made him happier.

———

Here are new opportunities for misery. Perhaps taking another road would have made *no* difference for David; even if he had married someone else, he would still hear that sorrowful music in the night. When we say, "even if . . . ," we make what the philosopher Nelson Goodman calls semifactual statements: you could have taken another road, and no doubt you think that's important, but really, it made no difference at all. Sometimes, this thought comes as a relief: if you've screwed up, you may be glad to learn it didn't matter. More often, though, semifactual thoughts are mocking. Even if you hadn't told your daughter to stay, she would have left. Even if you hadn't missed that date, he would have dumped you. Even if you hadn't hit "reply all," you wouldn't have gotten that contract. Some comfort. You're an *inconsequential* failure.

David's reflections about what might have been are only one instance of such speculation in a novel full of it. It's a regular feature of his married life. From their early flirtations (Dora: "Suppose you had never seen me at all"; David: "Suppose we had never been born!") through Dora's uninviting wedding-night question ("Are you happy now, you foolish boy . . . and sure you don't repent?") to her deathbed remarks ("I am afraid it would have been better, if we had only loved each other as a boy and girl, and forgotten it"), the couple ceaselessly compare David's life with its alternatives. Speculative comparison appears to have been his birthright, or perhaps a curse visited upon him. When he was born, his eccentric, witchy Aunt Betsey descended on the scene and, on discovering that David was a boy, became disgusted. She assumed that she would have a niece, and that this niece would be named, naturally, after her. "Where was this child's sister, Betsey Trotwood!" she exclaims, appalled. "Not forthcoming. Don't tell me!'" And yet, although little Betsey wasn't born, she does play a role in the novel; she tags along, as siblings will, with David as he grows up. She makes frequent forays into her god-mother's conversation, usually serving as an occasion for instructive comparison. "Come!" Aunt Betsey says to David at one point, "Your sister Betsey Trotwood would have told me what she thought of anyone, directly. Be as like your sister as you can, and speak out!" Unforthcoming, unreal little Betsey Trotwood is an ambassador in the novel for all that is excluded from it. She's the first of several characters present in the novel but not alive: David's half brother, who dies with his mother, David's own stillborn child, an older sister imagined by his friend, Steerforth. . . . By the end of his story, when David announces the existence of what he calls a "real live Betsey Trotwood"—that is, his daughter—his world has become crowded with people like Betsy, who don't exist.

Shortly after he is born, David maps out the metaphysical neighborhood of his youth, and gathers its inhabitants together in his mind:

> I lay in my basket, and my mother lay in her bed; but Betsey
> Trotwood Copperfield was for ever in the land of dreams
> and shadows, the tremendous region whence I had so lately
> traveled; and the light upon the window of our room shone
> out upon the earthly bourne of all such travelers, and the
> mound above the ashes and the dust that once was he,
> without whom I had never been.

Even as David thinks to inter Betsey in her own region—forever in the land of dreams and shadows, a region distinct from, if somehow adjacent to, the world in which he lives and the church-yard in which his father is buried—even as he inters her, she reminds him of his own contingency. That she will not be leads him to think that, had his father not been, he would not be. Thoughts of contingency are viral.

_____

All your houses are haunted by the person you might have been. The wraiths and phantoms creep under your carpets and between the warp and weft of your curtains, they lurk in wardrobes and lie flat under drawer-liners. You think of the child you might have had but didn't. When the midwife says, "It's a boy," where does the girl go? When you think you're pregnant and you're not, what happens to that child that was already formed in your mind? You keep it filed in a drawer in your consciousness, like a short story that wouldn't work after the opening lines.

—Hilary Mantel, *Giving Up the Ghost*

_____

Because fiction typically relies on the backward look of an authoritative, knowledgeable narrator, it naturally suggests that its representations are reliable. (Unreliable narrators exist, of course, but they get their interest from the norms of reliability they violate.) We take for granted that narrators, even first-person narrators such as David, know what they're talking about. But, again, in our lives we often don't know what has happened to us, much less what hasn't; so much has been hidden from us along our long, meandering path. The stories we tell manage this ignorance not by eliminating it, but by making it meaningful. (Sometimes this seems like making do.) Narrators organize the disarray of the past into a significant form, a plot.

In these plots, time comes in separate units, just as people do; unled lives foreground—indeed, make melodramatic—the idea of the *event*. From time's fluid movement one moment is chosen as the one that made all the difference. It's true that the conventions of our culture help: they've loaded some moments with consequence before our story begins. We've been told, for instance, as David was told, that our wedding will change everything for us. For Philip Larkin, this belief begged for derision:

To My Wife

Choice of you shuts up that peacock-fan
The future was, in which temptingly spread
All that elaborative nature can.
Matchless potential! but unlimited
Only so long as I elected nothing;
Simply to choose stopped all ways up but one,
And sent the tease-birds from the bushes flapping.
No future now. I and you now, alone.

So for your face I have exchanged all faces,
For your few properties bargained the brisk
Baggage, the mask-and-magic-man's regalia.
Now you become my boredom and my failure,
Another way of suffering, a risk,
A heavier-than-air hypostasis.

Marriage has reduced Larkin's speaker to extravagance, to puns and wordplay and ostentatious diction. Its sterility has ripened his cynicism. Spread / unlimited, nothing / flapping, one / alone, regalia / failure: the poem's off-rhymes tell my ears that these people are badly matched. This in a sonnet, the poetic form for love. I'm relieved to remember that Larkin never married, unsurprised to learn that he sometimes conducted four affairs at once.

———

"We may define a cause," wrote David Hume long ago, "to be an object, followed by another, and where all the objects similar to the first are followed by objects similar to the second. Or in other words where, if the first object had not been, the second never had existed." How do you know whether this event caused that one? Well, imagine the first event struck out of your life, as Pip says, and think how different the life to follow would have been. We understand how way leads to way by imagining ways untaken. We invent alternatives to tap and test the links between this event and that one. Sometimes the alternatives we imagine are fantastic and aimed to provoke our own dumbstruck wonder: "Captain, we cannot send him back: if we alter the past, the Enterprise herself will cease to exist!" But even the best of these stories—I think of Borges's "The Garden of Forking Paths," for instance—can seem merely clever.

It is easy to think that events gain their significance by what they cause, or by what has caused them; little things, after all, can make all the difference. But what has come to strike me, as I have read these stories, is how often they remind us that meaning comes in other ways than by causation—that the events of our lives are linked more imaginatively and intricately. Here's Larkin again:

Reference Back

That was a pretty one, I heard you call
From the unsatisfactory hall

To the unsatisfactory room where I
Played record after record, idly,
Wasting my time at home, that you
Looked so much forward to.

Oliver's *Riverside Blues*, it was. And now
I shall, I suppose, always remember how
The flock of notes those antique negroes blew
Out of Chicago air into
A huge remembering pre-electric horn
The year after I was born
Three decades later made this sudden bridge
From your unsatisfactory age
To my unsatisfactory prime.

Truly, though our element is time,
We are not suited to long perspectives
Open at each instant of our lives.
They link us to our losses: worse,
They show us what we have as it once was,
Blindingly undiminished, just as though
By acting differently we could have kept it so.

King Oliver's recording of "Riverside Blues" makes a bridge from the musicians in 1923 to Larkin and his mother in their separate rooms, and makes a bridge between her age and his prime; and Larkin's memory, then, makes another bridge from that moment to the present moment of his writing; and his poem makes a bridge to the present moment of my reading and, now, to yours. Bridges large and small span Larkin's recording of the past—the rhyme that cantilevers from "prime" to "time" over the second stanza break, the curious falling away and return of rhyme in the third stanza. I've convinced myself that as we read the line, "The flock of notes those antique negroes blew," our eyes bridge "flock" and "blew" to form "flew," a word present but unseen, present as the notes that flew out from the musicians' instruments are present, present as the past is present in music, present invisibly.

Larkin salutes the rambunctious potential of Oliver's polyphony: it's the very sound of possibility. And yet, he says, in bridging time's river, this recording has led us astray. It has let us think that we could have kept the past as it was, had we acted differently. But there's nothing we could have done. Thinking otherwise—thinking that we could have prevented time's diminishment—merely flatters us. Larkin liked the doubly draining word "undiminished" and used it later in "Sad Steps," where he speaks of "the strength and pain / Of being young; that it can't come again, / But is for others undiminished somewhere." That we're defined by loss is a dour thought, characteristic of the poet. For myself, though, I'd like to think that something is sometimes gained. The bridge in "Riverside Blues" is formed by Johnny Dodds's clarinet and Honore Dutray's trombone; when we cross over to the verse, we hear the trumpet of young Louis Armstrong, playing as if in Jericho.

———

When talking about the alternate pasts we create for ourselves, Kahneman and Tversky spoke of "mentally undoing" past events— *mentally* undoing because we can't *actually* undo them: they're irrevocable. But again, poems and stories about our unled lives test this easy assumption, ask us whether it is true that, as we say, past is past.

Salute

JAMES SCHUYLER

Past is past, and if one
remembers what one meant
to do and never did, is
not to have thought to do
enough? Like that gather-
ing of one of each I
planned, to gather one
of each kind of clover,
daisy, paintbrush that
grew in that field the cabin stood in and
study them one afternoon
before they wilted. Past
is past. I salute
that various field.

"Past is past": the word "past" returns in the very line that says it
doesn't, and, in returning, it brings a new meaning: past (that
time) is past (has gone by). So, we might say: past is past; past is
not past. No surprise that the phrase "Past is past" returns at the
poem's end, and no surprise that it means something new. At the
start of the poem, the phrase was a cliché, something anybody
would say; now, at the poem's end, it has become something exceptional, said by this one speaker in this one state of mind. The
past does and doesn't stay with us. It remains the same and doesn't
remain the same. In this way, Schuyler's elegant, paradoxical
poem tells us two things at once: $n + 1$.

This recollection of the past is and is not a new collection of
individual flowers brought together, a "gather-/ing." Arranging

his past, Schuyler revives it. And in doing so, he asks whether gathering flowers in his words makes up for not having gathered them in his hands. I imagine him wondering:

What is
enough

Perhaps this gathering of words—each exceptional, each commonplace—supplements the gathering of flowers the poet thought to have gathered; perhaps this unwilting bouquet of clover, daisy, paintbrush offers adequate recompense.

———

"Simply to choose stopped all ways up but one," Larkin wrote. Experience is exclusive. And it's irrevocable: "it can't come again." These are the central ideas tested by plots of unled lives. Is this poesy a posy? Is past past? Unsurprisingly these two qualities of plots—exclusiveness and irrevocability—are more amply evident in fiction and film than in poetry. We've seen as much in *It's a Wonderful Life*, where each episode forms a link in a chain. Chains represent experience as single and unchangeable: they're forged, and we're bound. It would take supernatural, or artistic, powers to free us.

Like *It's a Wonderful Life*, Max Ophüls's *Letter from an Unknown Woman* constructs an episodic plot from a linked chain of separate events. Having received a challenge from an aggrieved husband, Stefan Brand (Louis Jourdan), a dissolute pianist and debonair coward, prepares to bolt. He tells his mute manservant John (Art Smith) to pack his things and have a cab ready. John then hands him a note that begins, "By the time you read this letter, I may be dead. . . ." The film that follows is largely the projection of this letter's contents. (Yet another work of art posing as a familiar letter.) Again, like *It's a Wonderful Life*, *Letter from an Unknown Woman* unspools a sequence of episodes that show a life's exclusions. Those episodes tell the story of Lisa Berndl's (Joan Fontaine) infatuation with Brand from the day in her childhood when he moved into her apartment building, through her young adulthood when she followed his career, to their one-night affair, his disappearance, the birth of their child, the melancholy security of her proper marriage to an older man, and finally Brand's fatal return.

Ophüls, writes the film scholar Dan Morgan, "is not a director of the counterfactual." But he is *pointedly* not such a director: he rejects possibilities only after having raised them. *Letter from an Unknown Woman*, no less than *It's a Wonderful Life*, gives us a series of turning points, but turning points at which nothing happens. Brand fails to fall in love with Lisa over and over. Questions arise again as to whether the principal man and woman in this film are exceptional or anybody; whether they are free or bound, separate or united; whether chance or choice governs their lives. These motifs cycle by under the servant John's watchful eye: he knows the truth of this story but can't speak it, a mute god presiding over events he can't alter.

What most people remember about the film is its voice-over: Lisa's voice reads the letter that Brand grips in his hands, and the past she describes magically appears before us. As in Capra's movie, the past is a film. And, again, our experience is often split between what we see and what we hear: our eyes see Lisa in the past, our ears hear her voice in the present, sounding invisibly in Brand's head. Once more, the voice of an angel punctuates the movie we watch, like a celestial director's commentary track. In Ophüls's film, it's Lisa's voice we hear, and it comes not from heaven but from the grave. It's as if vision allowed us access to this world, while hearing allowed access to other realms, above and below—to the music of the spheres and the Orphic underworld. It's true that for stretches of the film her voice-over is silent and the characters of her past speak for themselves. But often, we can't hear them. They drift away from the camera, into and out of earshot, sometimes visible through windows and palings, at other times mingling inaudibly with street musicians. The effect is a strange sense of estrangement: past and present are pulling apart, have pulled apart. Time is broken, and the movie strains its syntax to comprehend.

It might seem that Brand has made a bad decision—that it would have been better had he asked Lisa to marry him. But he doesn't make decisions; he drifts on easy pleasures. For him to have decided not to be with her would have been a moral accomplishment. As it is, he's never truly even seen her. With a nice sense of irony, Ophüls makes the decisive recognition not his but hers: if we've been waiting sentimentally for Brand to fall in love with Lisa, what happens is that she finally realizes that he's unworthy of her. Before sending her letter, Lisa came to offer herself to him, only to see that he had no clue who she was. She's the one who has made disastrous choices.

The final irony of the movie, however, is that its most dramatic crisis is not any of the many episodes in which Brand fails to awaken to the promise of this young woman before him, nor even the moment when she realizes that she's misspent her life. Instead, it's the event we ourselves have seen and heard, his reading of her letter: the two-hour movie itself is one long turning point. If we've forgotten the movie's first scene then we, too, have missed it. We've been no more alert than Brand. For, by the time he has finished reading, his seconds have arrived. John silently escorts him out the front door, into a dark dawn, for his appointment with Lisa's husband, an unerring marksman.

———

> None of us has time to live the true dramas of the life that we are destined for. This is what ages us—this, and nothing else. The wrinkles and creases in our faces are the registration of the great passions, vices, insights that called on us; but we, the masters, were not at home.
>
> —Walter Benjamin, on "the Image of Proust"

———

When a novel or film has a single plot, it tends to highlight the irrevocable nature of the past more than its exclusiveness. Capra does encourage us to compare George Bailey's fate with that of his brother, his friend Sam, and Potter; and Ophüls does encourage us to compare Lisa's life of grisaille propriety with the brilliant life she might have led with Brand. But in both films the feeling of life's irrevocability is more powerful than the feeling of its exclusivity. George's birth and Lisa's death form the foundation of their films, and neither can be undone.

By contrast, multiplot novels orchestrate events as irrevocable and exclusive with a more even hand, and often on an immense scale. Especially in their elaborately assured nineteenth-century form, they are exhaustive studies of the aesthetic and emotional possibilities offered by the pasts we invent. Here are the opening sentences of Anthony Trollope's *He Knew He Was Right*: "When Louis Trevelyan was twenty-four years old, he had all the world before him where to choose; and, among other things, he chose to go to the Mandarin Islands, and there fell in love with Emily Rowley, the daughter of Sir Marmaduke, the governor." Conceiving of all that is to come as a continuation of *Paradise Lost*—where Adam and Eve also have the world before them, where to choose—Trollope prepares us for his extensive treatment of choice as it is worked out in that main event of the courtship novel, marital choice, and prepares us as well for a study of the consequences of such choices. That choices are made in an emphatically fallen world, Gabriel's flaming brand warming our backs, is soon clear enough. Married within three pages, Trevelyan suspects his wife of infidelity within four, and across the following 919 Emily must endure Trevelyan opening her letters, calling her a harlot, hiring a detective to spy on her, throwing her out of the house, and abducting their child—while Trevelyan, tormented by his thoughts, drives away not only his wife but all his friends, flees his country, isolates himself, and descends, finally, into alcoholic decrepitude, madness, and death. Emily and Trevelyan are trapped in themselves, and in their marriage. The claustrophobia of their plot is almost unbearable (for them, for us). It's a desperate tale, extraordinary among those written by canonical Victorian realists, in which the web of daily practices—visits paid, letters written, servants instructed, conversations entertained—turns gossamer and fails, and we find ourselves abruptly plunged into the arid Italian countryside, alone with a mad, drunken, dying hero.

This plummeting decline is necessary, for Trollope wants all the other choices in the novel to be made in the shadow cast by this one. And there are many others: *He Knew He Was Right* is pullulating with proposals. Emily's sister Nora twice refuses the decent, gentlemanly, future peer Mr. Glascock before accepting penniless Hugh Stanbury; Hugh's sister Dorothy refuses the hand of the fatuous clergyman Mr. Gibson before accepting Brooke Burgess; and Mr. Gibson, both before and after his proposal to

Dorothy, makes love to a pair of indistinguishable sisters, proposing to (and being accepted by) each of them in turn. Trollope is a connoisseur of such proposals. You can see his eyes narrow, his attention sharpen, his pleasure mount, as he sees one coming his way down the plot: the forward propulsion of his text is suddenly slowed by an awareness of alternatives, plot becomes a matter of forking options, and our narrator settles down to enjoy the satisfactions of psychological analysis and emotional manipulation.

Mr. Glasscock sits quietly before Nora Rowley, absently tapping his cane on the ground, while she reflects on his generous offer and Trollope lovingly unfurls the interplay of all that shapes her reflections: the physical presence of his body, to which she would get yet closer should she say yes; her appreciation of his character, graceful spirit, and actions; her necessarily hasty reassessment of her feelings toward him (does she love him?); her recollection of his wealth and status; the needs and hopes of her family; the assumptions of her society; her beliefs about the nature of woman's lot; her youthful dreams of what marriage might be; the courteous words she has just heard; her determination to say yes; and throughout these dreamlike deliberations, the brute fact of the passage of time, the cane gently tapping and then tapping again, until Nora finds herself, against all reason, finally saying no.

Trollope is shameless in extracting the rewards to be had from reminding us of all that was once possible for his characters. Thus, after Mr. Glasscock proposes to her, after she declines, and after he leaves, we're told that Nora immediately

> began to think in earnest of what she had done. If the reader were told that she regretted the decision which she

had been forced to make so rapidly, a wrong impression would be given of the condition of her thoughts. But there came upon her suddenly a strange capacity for counting up and making a mental inventory of all that might have been hers. She knew—and where is the girl so placed that does not know?—that it is a great thing to be an English peeress. . . . She had been taught from a very early age that all the material prosperity of her life must depend on matrimony. She could never be comfortably disposed of in the world, unless some fitting man who possessed those things of which she was so bare, should wish to make her his wife. Now there had come a man so thoroughly fitting, so marvelously endowed, that no worldly blessing would have been wanting. Mr. Glascock had more than once spoken to her of the glories of Monkhams. She thought of Monkhams now more than she had ever thought of the place before. It would have been a great privilege to be the mistress of an old time-honoured mansion, to call oaks and elms her own, to know that acres of gardens were submitted to her caprices, to look at herds of cows and oxen, and be aware that they lowed on her own pastures. And to have been the mother of a future peer of England, to have the nursing, and sweet custody and very making of a future senator,—would not that have been much?

To be mistress of Monkhams might be something! But, "let it be as it might," we're told, "she was destroyed." It's not enough for Nora to entertain such thoughts; her sister Emily, her mother, and her father do so as well: standing slack-jawed before all that is now beyond Nora's reach becomes a melancholy family pastime.

The thought of all that he had lost, of all that might so easily have been his, for a time overwhelmed Sir Marmaduke. . . . He could understand that a girl should not marry a man whom she did not like; but he could not understand how any girl should not love such a suitor as was Mr. Glascock. . . . He went out and thought of it all, and felt as though Paradise had been opened to his child and she had refused to enter the gate.

Such comparisons of marital possibilities occur in all the plots of Trollope's novel, as when Hugh's sister Dorothy must consider whether to remain unmarried or to marry Mr. Gibson, who has been urged on her by her loving and stubborn aunt; or as when that aunt finds herself wondering whether it is better "for a young woman to look forward to the cares and affections, and perhaps hard usage, of a married life; or to devote herself to the easier and safer course of an old maid's career." When the characters themselves don't compare their alternatives and consequences, the narrator does it for them. "Had he gone to her now and said a word to her in gentleness all might have been made right," we're told during a quarrel between Emily and Trevelyan. "But he did not go to her." I could multiply examples, but perhaps the point has been made: Trollope loves unled lives and loves what they offer him by way of suspense and torqued feelings. So contagious is his enthusiasm that readers caught it: in *He Knew He Was Right,* remarked the *Times,* "Mr. Trollope has never given a better illustration of all he is and all he is not."

In a single-plot novel like *Persuasion* the experience of being shackled by a chain of iron or gold, thorns or flowers, is mainly a temporal phenomenon. Regret and relief are the dominant feelings. *He Knew He Was Right* certainly studies the way that the

undone endures: we've just seen Nora ward off the regret it invites. Never one to let conventions go unexploited, Trollope makes
the most of the hackneyed question of whether a woman's "no"
truly means no, in order to ratchet up the intensity of regret.
Having been refused once, Mr. Glascock gives Nora another opportunity to say yes and Trollope an opportunity to have her say
no once more. "You refused him then—a second time?" Nora's
father asks, dumbfounded. But Trollope most powerfully makes
this point about the irrevocability of experiences as he makes
most of his points in the novel, through comparison. Nora's
second offer only makes more poignant the contrasting experience of her sister Emily, who has no second chance but must endure a life beached on the aftermath of her first. "For myself,"
she remarks, "if I could begin life again, I do not think that any
temptation would induce me to place myself in a man's power."
But, of course, she can't begin life again.

This whirlwind of regret and relief, sympathy and envy, drives
Trollope's characters to extravagant passions, to thinking of
themselves as epic heroes and as dogs, to grandiose dreams of
transcendent power and despairing thoughts of annihilation, to
knife-wielding rage and ludicrous humiliation. From the familiar
plot of romance, Trollope creates the most extreme effects. Sometimes this extremity seems lunatic: it's when he is descending
into madness that Trevelyan cries, "Change of everything; I want
change of everything. . . . If I could have a new body and a new
mind, and a new soul!" But to say that it's lunatic isn't to say it's
uncommon. In some moods the mere thought of others is hellish.

CHAPTER TWO

Tales of Our Adulthood

I f imagining the lives I haven't led grows out of my feeling of singularity as I travel down one path among many, then situations that make me confront either my singularity or those many paths are most likely to engender thoughts of unled lives. And so, my question becomes, when do I feel limited irrevocably and exclusively to myself, just like everyone else? The answers to this question are historical and social as well as personal. The road Frost's traveler chose had been beaten and worn by others before him.

———

In the late eighteenth century, writes the philosopher Charles Taylor, there emerged an enduring psychological tension in Western reflection on the nature and experience of the self. On the one hand, people came to believe that they had within themselves deep sources of identity, bottomless depths of thought, imagination, and memory—depths that set them apart from other people. On the other hand, they could also haul themselves up from that deep selfhood and look impersonally at themselves and others, at their lives and at the lives of others. They could rise to an elevated position and make their comparisons. Together, these contradictory habits of self-immersion and abstracted comparison form what Taylor calls the modern "subject with depth," for whom the thought of alternate possibilities comes naturally. We believe that we have "an original path which we ought to tread," he remarks—but which one is it?

As this understanding of the self has come to seem natural, the number of paths apparently available has increased. In a "posttraditional social universe," writes the sociologist Anthony Giddens, "an indefinite range of potential courses of action . . . is at any given moment open." The reticulation of possibilities—the increased number of forks in any road—has transformed our understanding of the course of any single life. "Choosing among such alternatives," writes Giddens, "is always an 'as if' matter, a question of selecting [among] 'possible worlds.' Living in circumstances of modernity is best understood as a matter of the routine contemplation" of such alternatives. But it's no less true that "living in circumstances of modernity" brings an increased exposure to things that happen unchosen: risk and chance no less than choice have come to shape our experience.

The main engine driving this modern experience has no doubt been market capitalism, with its isolation of individuals and its accelerating generation of choices and chances, molding behavior in ever-increasing ways. It's not that no one had imagined other lives for themselves before the first cotton factory was built or Adam Smith wrote *The Wealth of Nations,* but such lives have been nursed by an economic system that isolates us and urges us to calculate opportunities and maximize their effects. The elevation of choice as an absolute good, the experience of chance as a strange affront, the increasing number of exciting, stultifying decisions we must make, the review of the past to improve future outcomes: they all feed the people we're not. It's no wonder that the study of alternative pasts has flourished in business schools. Sitting at dinner with a British economist, I talk about Charles Dickens, the plots of his stories, and the inner lives of his characters. "Who," my fellow diner donnishly inquires, "will benefit from your research outcomes?" Pause. "Executives, perhaps."

But if modern capitalist markets have bred our unled lives, more particular historical and social conditions explain their changing power decade by decade. Or, rather, it's the interaction of those shifting conditions and the enduring variations of the story form I've been studying that explains that power. A self with inner depths, alive at once to its uniqueness and its commonness, inclined to retrospection and comparison, ready to see what's not, traveling down a narrow one-way street: what, at this moment or that, would encourage someone to think of themselves like this?

Historians speak of the rise of modern professional society in the nineteenth century. Unlike the agricultural and industrial societies that preceded it, professional society has been made up of specialized careers, ladders of achievement dependent not on inherited property or on amassed capital but on individual capacities and training. In Britain especially, the professional became a dominant social type. More people came to think of themselves as having, or potentially having, a career. But at the same time, these professions developed rigid boundaries, what the historian

Harold Perkin drily calls "strategies of enclosure," often in the form of tests designed to keep people out. Ideally inclusive, professions are practically exclusive. They differ from each other in particulars. Salary, prestige, workday, security, independence, and relation to the state all vary among doctors, military professionals, businesspeople, ministers, professors, civil servants, lawyers, judges, journalists. . . . "All professionals are equal but some are more equal than others," as Perkin puts it. The result is "a collection of parallel hierarchies of unequal height, each with its own ladder of many rungs."

The conditions for unled lives are in place. Instead of a road you have a ladder, and instead of walking you climb. Choosing one ladder means you haven't chosen another: to choose to be a lawyer is to choose not to be a doctor or a banker. In this way, you separate yourself from everyone else and clamber up into your future. Of course, you can change ladders, but it's hard work: you must start from the ground once again. And so you climb on, head down, placing your feet on the rungs, first one than the other, while people around you do the same thing.

———

Whether a young man enters business or the ministry may depend on a decision which has to be made before a certain day. He takes the place offered in the counting-house, and is committed. Little by little, the habits, the knowledges, of the other career, which once lay so near, cease to be reckoned even among his possibilities. At first, he may sometimes doubt whether the self he murdered in that decisive hour might not have been the better of the two; but with the years such questions themselves expire, and the

old alternative ego, once so vivid, fades into something less
substantial than a dream.

—William James, "Great Men and Their Environment"

Some careers encourage the imagination of unlived lives more
than others. I've been saying that authorship and filmmaking are
two of these. The law is another. To cast doubt on the allegations
made about her client, a defense lawyer presents alternatives. You
say my client has performed these acts, committed this crime.
Perhaps. But consider these possibilities: that he was in fact elsewhere, that the crime was committed with another weapon, that
this other suspect had greater motive. . . . It's no surprise, given
Dickens's preoccupation with lives unled, that he loved writing
about lawyers. In *Great Expectations,* Mr. Jaggers takes rooms
deep in the novel and there cultivates an aura of mystical power
by imagining alternate pasts for his clients. He's a storyteller.

But it isn't just that some careers invite thoughts of careers untaken: all careers do. As a young person, you stand before your
options and weigh them. If you're lucky, these options have come
to you full of promise. You imagine what each of them might hold
for you—and as you do, the trap springs. You find that you have
committed yourself to dissatisfaction, for these present, imagined
alternatives will become unlived pasts. Standing before a fork in
your road, you picture where each path might take you, and pave
the way to regret. In this way careers are unlike vocations. You're
called to a vocation because it expresses your essence, who you
are. To wish for another vocation is to wish not for change but
for replacement. But the career, not the vocation, is the typically
modern form of work.

No surprise, then, that one of the recurrent character types in modern literature is the young man frozen in the face of his options, unwilling to settle on any of the careers available to him. Nineteenth-century fiction made such scenes of privileged indecision a minor specialty: Stendhal, Balzac, Flaubert, Thackeray, Eliot, Hardy all played variations on them. Hugh Stanbury, in Trollope's *He Knew He Was Right,* hesitates between the law and journalism. Richard Carstone, in Dickens's *Bleak House,* dabbles in medicine and then the law and then the army before going mad. These young men want to keep the cup in their hand, rattling the dice. Who can blame them? Who would chase after regret?

———

Richard Carstone might have drifted through various professions before he died, but the woman he loved, Ada Clare, could choose only to marry or not to marry. Some nineteenth-century women, of course, didn't have that choice. Perhaps Ada might have become a governess—one of the few paths open to middle-class women. Among the ironies of Victorian "governess novels" was the way their authors found opportunities in the opportunities their heroines lacked. In Mrs. Henry Wood's *East Lynne*—a transatlantic sensation as a novel, as innumerable stage productions, and later as English, American, Australian, and Tamilese films—Lady Isabel Carlyle leaves her husband and children for a charming and deceptive rake, only to be disfigured beyond recognition in a patently retributive train wreck. Tortured by remorse, she returns to her husband to find that he, believing her dead, has remarried. "To see him—my husband—the husband of another!" she cries, "It is killing me." And it does. But not before we enjoy many pages that describe her life as a governess for her own children, a stranger in her own home, haunting the life she might have led, the marriage she might have enjoyed, the family she might have openly loved. (In one of the stage adaptations Lady Isabel stands with her dead son draped across her arms, looks to the audience, and wails, "Gone! And never called me mother!") For Wood, it was a mark of our fallen perversity that even love is most sharply felt vicariously. "To live in this house with your wife," Lady Isabel says to her husband as she finally dies, "to see your love for her; to watch the envied caresses that once were mine! I never loved you so passionately as I have done since I lost you."

Lady Isabel's situation may seem extreme, but Wood, a deeply Christian writer, meant it to represent ordinary life. When she herself died, her son wrote that her purpose was "to set forth the doctrine of good and evil; to point out the two paths in life, and the consequences that must follow the adoption of either."

It's a small sign of the complexity of historical and literary change that while governesses have become largely extinct, governess novels have survived. Claire Messud's *The Woman Upstairs* is a story of a young, cultured woman, forced by poverty, the lack of a family, and the cultural constraints of her society to be a teacher and babysitter. Her mother has died from Lou Gehrig's disease. It took years: her body became "a prison, one closing door after another, until she was confined inside her mind—a room, it is true, with no walls, but ultimately with no doors, either." Now, the daughter, Nora, is trapped within her own doorless life, in danger of dying into herself. She's thirty-seven, "a time of reckoning, the time at which you acknowledge once and for all that your life has a shape and a horizon, and that you'll probably never be president, or a millionaire, and that if you're a childless woman, you will quite possibly remain that way." Once, she thought she would become an artist in a paint-smudged smock, with an airy studio and children playing in the garden. Now, she's given up those expectations. She has become "a woman without notable surprises," a teacher, "the favorite teacher of the Appleton Elementary third-grade class," tending others' children, standing off to one side in all the photos, a star consigned to a small role.

> Which one is Nora? I can't quite picture her . . .
> You know, that nice third-grade teacher—not the one with the cotton candy hair, the other one.
> That's who I'm supposed to be, the other one: "No, not the really great artist in that studio, the other one."
> "Not the beautiful woman in the knockout dress—the other one."
> "The funny one?"
> "Oh, yeah, I guess she's that. The funny one."

"I'm not exactly not an artist," Nora says, "and I don't exactly not have children." She's an artist manqué, a mother manqué, a person manqué, and she has decided that this, simply, is what life is. Life manqué.

Into this diminished world arrive the Shahids, wife, husband, and son, just in from Paris. Skandar is visiting Harvard for the year, Sirena is working on her art, Reza is a student in Nora's class, and Nora is in love with all of them. She quotes Larkin: "On me your voice falls, as they say love should—like an enormous 'yes.'" Everything old is new: the wind picks up and she can feel it on her skin. She comes to think again that she is special, precious. "Everything hinges on this time," she says, "and nothing will be the same again." But it's hard to enter a family. She sleeps with Skandar, imagines an affair with Sirena, and babysits for the son. ("A son, my son," she thinks.) As we're told at one point, Nora is *like* an auntie, a mother, a wife, a lover, a governess. She participates in the family, metaphorically. Which is also to say she's a reader, metaphorically, living impossibly close to a world *like* her own—until she doesn't and the novel ends.

––––––––

The conditions of professional society are changing for men and women both. If, as sociologists report, more people are sustaining two careers at once or having several careers across the course of their working lives, then perhaps the memory of career choice will prompt fewer thoughts of careers untaken. The sense of a career as something exclusive and irrevocable will fade. For millennials, it already has faded. But for the moment, the decline of the career has seemed only to intensify our experience of unled working lives. The very studies that investigate those changing conditions do so in familiar terms. We're told by the sociologist Barry Schwartz, for instance, that most workers would choose a different career if they could start again; that the proliferation of possible careers has made choosing one a stupefying ordeal; and that to change careers you should first develop "branching projects," alternatives to be tested in your spare time while considering whether to leave your main path.

––––––––

"A man chooses his career at an age when he is not fit to choose," Nietzsche wrote. "He doesn't know the various professions; he doesn't know himself; and then he wastes his most active years in this career, giving his whole mind to it, acquiring experience." Our choices, such as they are, are made in ignorance. Looking back, thinking how much we know now, we think how little we knew then. In this, Nietzsche writes, careers are like love: "successful cases, like successful marriages, are exceptions, and even these are not the result of reason."

Marriage is in its way a career, and like a career, it offers clear sight lines to left and right. But marriage is a more urgent occasion for unlived lives than a career is, in part, because most of us believe marriage is more central to who we are. But it's also more urgent because it better suits the form taken by stories of unlived lives. Like a career, but more dramatically, marriage is exclusive: in marrying one person, you don't marry many others. Like a career, but more dramatically, marriage is costly to leave. (Before divorce was legal, of course, leaving was impossible.) And like a career, marriage stretches into the distant future—not merely till retirement, but till death do you part. If you do part— if you divorce, separate or slowly fall out of love—your singularity can return with crushing force.

———

In the collection *Stag's Leap*, Sharon Olds reconsiders her marriage. Her husband has left her, and she can't comprehend what has happened. "How could it be," she writes in "September 2001, New York City,"

> that he is, now,
> unknown to me, unseen by me,
> unheard by me, untouched by me,
> but known by others, seen by others,
> heard, touched.

"Minute by minute, I do not get up and just/go to him," she writes in "Not Going to Him."

> It is what I do now: not go, not
> see or touch. And after eleven
> million six hundred sixty-four thousand
> minutes of not, I am a stunned knower
> of not.

He is unknown, unseen, unheard, untouched; she does not go, does not see or touch. Reading the poems, you hear the waters pull away from Olds, leaving her stranded, alone, undone.

Although Olds's solitary knowledge of not is unwordable, she tries to word it anyway. She compares losing her husband not with death, which you might expect, but with outliving. Olds was not "driven/against the grate of a mortal life, but/just the slowly shut gate/of preference." "When my husband left," she writes,

> there was a pain I did not
> feel, which those who lose the one
> who loves them feel.

Olds's husband didn't die. But perhaps, Olds imagines, he felt he was dying; perhaps, for him, leaving the marriage meant entering life. In "Pain I Did Not," she writes,

> if
> he had what it took to rip his way out, with his
> teeth, then he could be born.

It's a brutal image and a confusing one. It makes of their marriage a body, in which they lived together, like twins in a mother's womb. But since I know from other poems that Olds is herself a mother, and has borne children fathered by this man, she seems to be within the marriage while the marriage is also within her, perhaps in the womb of her memory. In any case, it's hard not to see his self-delivery as a violence against her.

From that bloody, body-felt metaphor, Olds recoils into the comparative safety of abstraction. But her thoughts remain confusing:

> And so he went
> into another world—this
> world, where I do not see or hear him

How is the truth to be said? Stunned knower of not, Olds doesn't see, doesn't hear him in this world that is somehow also another world. Although her tone has become milder, I still feel the work she's performing. She is feeling and thinking very hard, working within herself and on herself. I imagine it's like having your hand on your womb, feeling both inside and out an elbowing child.

———

I'm talking with a friend on a summer's evening in California. We've arranged to be by ourselves and sit side by side. The shadow of a jacaranda tree, the smell of eucalyptus, the approach of mist, twilight in everything: a day done. Nothing remarkable. But then I realize my friend has brought me here so she can tell me that she and her husband have decided to separate, perhaps divorce. Neither has yet moved out of the small house they share. They're separate together in the place where they've been together together, and their past is present all around them. The relationship they do not now have is the most real thing in the house. It is insistent; it fills and empties her. She can't bear it any more, is helpless, and has panic attacks. She cries and cries. People pass by, looking into the darkness.

———————

"If you marry, you will regret it," wrote Kierkegaard. "If you do not marry, you will also regret it; if you marry or do not marry, you will regret both." Kierkegaard's bleak humor was matched a little later in his century by that of Thomas Hardy, poet of gutted hope. His poems are a curiosity cabinet of implausible failures:

A woman stands over the grave of her ex-husband. Across the grave stands the man's second wife. Musing over her past, the first wife regrets that she divorced him, and wishes instead that the three of them could have lived together, "like wives in the patriarch's days." ("Over the Coffin")

An unwed girl is pregnant, deserted by her lover. One Sunday morning, the girl's distraught mother gives her some herbs she thinks will cause an abortion. The girl and her unborn child die, just as the lover returns, now ready to marry her. The mother regrets that she herself hasn't died. ("A Sunday Morning Tragedy")

An aged, impoverished man must suffer the indignity of going to live in the workhouse. The rules dictate that he and his wife sleep apart, but the curate takes pity on him and allows them to sleep together. Unfortunately, sleeping apart from his wife was the one thing the man looked forward to. ("A Curate's Kindness")

God, found grieving after the extinction of all life, explains
that He regrets having created the world ("By the Earth's
Copse"). It's hard to know whether this poem is more or
less dismal than "God-Forgotten," in which the world and
all its inhabitants have slipped His immortal mind altogether. "By Me created?" He asks, vaguely.

In chimney nook after chimney nook, Hardy's imagination
bears its stillborn children. It's the fertility of his regret that's
extraordinary, the dogged ingenuity with which he invents occasions to think of all that is not—of all that "unbe," as he strain-
ingly puts it. The critic James Richardson has pointed out that the
evacuating prefix is chronic. From the volume *Wessex Poems*
alone: "unsoothed," "unchosen," "unshent," "unsight," "unaware,"
"unwitting," "unconscious," "unheed," "undoubting," "unseemly,"
"uneven," "unpaid," "unbroken," "unspoken," "unrest," "unwont-
edly," and "undistrest." Hardy is a poet not of absence but of sub-
traction, a poet of $n-1$.

——————

But it was marriage—his own marriage—that most reliably pro-
pelled Hardy's backpedaling imagination. While visiting Corn-
wall as a young man, he met Emma Gifford and within a few
weeks was writing her love lyrics. In one of these, "Ditty," he proclaims his devotion by describing not how wonderful it is to be
with her, nor how painful it would be to be without her, but how
painful it would be to be without her and not know what he was
missing in missing her.

> To feel I might have kissed—
>   Loved as true—

Otherwhere, nor Mine have missed
   My life through,
Had I never wandered near her,
Is a smart severe.

Emma, unsurprisingly, found this a little chilly. But the senti-
ment was characteristic of her fiancée: Hardy sharpened his
feelings on the steel of their contingency. The compacted recognition of what is and what is not served him better as a poet
than as a lover; it fermented his ironies. Reading his poems,
Richardson remarks, "We are forced to recognize simultaneously
how irrevocably things are what they are and how easily they
could have been otherwise"—as straightforward a description
of our singularity as one could want. But not a wooing sort of
thought.

But that doesn't mean to say, of course, there aren't occasions now and then—extremely desolate occasions—when
you think to yourself: "What a terrible mistake I've made
with my life." And you get to thinking about a different life,
a better life you might have had. For instance, I get to
thinking about a life I may have had with you, Mr. Stevens.

—Kazuo Ishiguro, *The Remains of the Day*

It's true that the irrevocability and exclusivity of marriage recom-
mend it to the imagination of unlived lives. But there's a more interesting, and more painful, reason that there are so many marriages in our stories. The Bible and its culture tell us that marrying
someone means you're no longer one person, separate from others,

but are now one person with your spouse, "one flesh." In stories of lives unled, coupledom is imagined as being not two people but one compound person, for better or for worse. The failure of a marriage, or the failure to get married if you believe that to be a failure, then can make your single life smaller and more unhappily confined. "Everybody, one might say, is left out of being someone else," as Adam Phillips remarks. "Coupledom is as close as you can get"—if you want it, can get it, and can keep it.

———

Toward the end of "Brokeback Mountain," Annie Proulx projects a quietly complex image of being "one flesh." Ennis Del Mar and Jack Twist had decades of not—not being married, not living together, not sharing a cabin on Brokeback Mountain. They met in the summer of 1963, when they were working on a ranch, neither yet twenty, both high school dropouts with no futures. But when they're on the mountain, they own the world. They don't talk about sex, but let it happen, denying being gay even though their summer meetings are when they are most alive.

They both marry women, have kids, find jobs, and across twenty years meet occasionally. They take things differently. Jack is haunted by the lives they might have led together, running a little ranch or living in Mexico, somewhere away from civilization and its systematic and personal violence. He tries to persuade Ennis to elope, but Ennis won't. "I'm stuck with what I got," he says,

> caught in my own loop. Can't get out of it. Jack, I don't want to be like them guys you see around sometimes. And I don't want a be dead. . . . There's nothing now we can do. . . . What I'm saying, Jack, I built a life up in them years. Love my little girls. Alma? Ain't her fault.

Ennis has no "serious hard feelings, just a vague sense of getting short changed." He's puzzled: "I been lookin at people on the street," he says, "This happen a other people?" Jack isn't puzzled; he's furious. "We could a had a good life together, a fuckin real good life," he says, but "you wouldn't do it, Ennis." All they have now is "years of things unsaid and now unsayable."

Before he's beaten to death with a tire iron, Jack remembers and craves

> the time that distant summer on Brokeback when Ennis had come up behind him and pulled him close, the silent embrace satisfying some shared and sexless hunger. They had stood that way for a long time in front of the fire, its burning tossing ruddy chunks of light, the shadow of their bodies a single column against the rock. . . . That dozy embrace solidified in his memory as the single moment of artless, charmed happiness in their separate and difficult lives.

All the features of our stories are here: travel, marriage, children, a lost life of joy, and at the end, this one image of single lives separately enclosed, but shadowed by an ecstatic unity of two as one.

———

The various forces engendering unled lives have shifted at different rates and interacted with each other in different ways over time. Some of the changes have been obvious, some obscure. This makes dating the history of their development difficult. Changes in the conditions of gay people have been so rapid in the past fifty years that they've sometimes seemed visible or audible. We can hear history dopplering away from us into the past. Between 1963, when "Brokeback Mountain" opens and 1997, when it was published, conditions changed radically; they changed further between then and now, and perhaps further yet between my writing and your reading. Yet Proulx's story remains recognizably one of ours.

———

The transformations of the relations between career and marriage have been similarly rapid and dramatic. (That speed, too, shapes our experience, of course: we remember our parents and measure our distance.) Meg Wolitzer opens her novel *The Interestings* by dating its first forking moment precisely: early July 1974, the summer that a helicopter lifted the former president away from the White House lawn. When a boy at camp miraculously and without apparent reason asks the novel's main character, Jules, to hang out with the cool kids, she says sure.

> What if she'd said *no*? she liked to wonder afterwards in a kind of strangely pleasurable, baroque horror. What if she'd turned down the lightly flung invitation and went about her life, thudding obliviously along like a drunk person, a blind person, a moron, someone who thinks that the small packet of happiness she carries is enough.

Through the course of the eighties, nineties, and oughts, through the onset of AIDS, the events of September 11th, the rise of New York real estate prices, all the novel's characters, straight and gay, male and female, shed one possibility after another. Jules does not marry Ethan, who loves her, and does not become an actress as she had hoped: like all her friends, she becomes the one person she ever is to be. The novel's conclusion is time-stamped with a precision that equals its opening. It's a time of Skype and "mastery seminars" and medical tourism and musicians living in Greenpoint. Now, more or less. The diminishment of Wolitzer's characters comes to seem the diminishment of a generation, my generation, the whittling away of all of us.

The choice of a career, the choice of a spouse or partner—memories of these choices may be the most common prompts of unled lives. But I believe that thoughts of our parents, siblings, and children pry more deeply into us. Their power, again, derives in part from the importance granted to family relations in our culture, from our vehemence and confusion. But, again, this power also derives from the way that the features of families accord with the story form we've been studying. Like having a career and marriage, being in a family sets you on a path that lasts until you die. It's exclusive and irrevocable: even death doesn't end it. More importantly, family relationships are powerful because, like marriage, they promise an escape from our singularity. When the family members are biologically related to you, the similarity of their bodies to yours can seem to confirm that hope. You see yourself outside yourself. But when children are adopted or carried by surrogacy, what might have been may still press. In the late 1990s Melissa Etheridge and her partner were looking for a sperm donor. Finally, they had to choose between two of their friends: David Crosby and Brad Pitt. Years later Etheridge told a reporter, "My teenagers now are like, 'I could have had Brad Pitt [as a father]. . . . I could've been amazingly handsome.'"

Because the relation of parent to child can make escaping ourselves seem possible, the death of a child, or the death of the chance to have a child, can cast us back into ourselves. In this, it's like the failure of a marriage, but often with more grief and consequence. In Emily Brontë's *Wuthering Heights*, Heathcliff's restless ambitions can be seen to derive from his condition as a replacement for another child, also called Heathcliff, but dead; in *East Lynne*, Lady Isabel's lamentations rain most heavily on her son's deathbed ("If I had not—done as I did—how different would it have been now!"); in Hardy's *Tess*, the death of Tess's son prepares her for the thought that death is preferable to life; in James's *The Ambassadors*, Strether's dull boy lies buried within his father's forlorn heart; in Rebecca West's *Return of the Soldier* we first meet our characters in a dead baby's sunlit nursery. The enduring agonies of these stories can be found more recently in Lionel Shriver's *The Post-Birthday World*, Mary Gordon's *The Love of My Youth*, Kate Atkinson's *Life after Life*, the novels of Elena Ferrante, and the poetry of Lucille Clifton and Rachel Zucker. They are so familiarly devastating in and out of literature that Lydia Davis can count on her readers to respond to them, even when she writes with her characteristically dry economy. Here's her story "A Double Negative" in its entirety: "At a certain point in her life, she realizes it is not so much that she wants to have a child as that she does not want not to have a child, or not to have had a child."

———

The changing conditions of marriage, professional life, and parenting have come together in recent decades to make this experience only more intense, especially for women. Committed to careers, mothers glance sideways at childless professional women, or they look at mothers who have left professional careers, or at working fathers who do little child-rearing. Mothers who have decided against a career, or have been unable to pursue one, look at the women around them who do work professionally. And women who cannot have children, or do not, look at those who do. There seems to be no right path; every good excludes others. "Here's the catch," Maggie Nelson says: *I cannot hold my baby at the same time as I write.* " Each sentence she writes, each sentence I read, silently tells me that she's not holding her baby—as if the cost of consequence were letting go. (When I first read this, I thought: *my book in a sentence.*)

If the family resemblance of bodies seems to promise an escape from yourself, the lack of resemblance denies that promise. Stories of racial passing naturally focus on this. Like Fauset's *Plum Bun,* such stories focus on figures who don't look like their black siblings, parents, or children. They have more choices and are exposed to a greater number of chances than their black family members. This is why they make good protagonists.

The unnamed narrator of James Weldon Johnson's *The Autobiography of an Ex-Colored Man* is a talented, light-skinned, biracial ragtime pianist and composer with professional dreams. He wants "to be a great man, a great colored man, to reflect credit on the race and gain fame." He tours through the North and the South and across Europe, travels among the working classes and the rich, the worlds of black people and white; his story is an expansive travelogue of cultures, written by a man who can participate in all of them while belonging to none. His very value as a narrator—his ability to guide us through these separate social worlds—comes from his unusual, indeterminate racial status. Even for him, though, growth hardens and excludes. As his story narrows to its close, he decides to marry a white woman and to give up his dreams of artistic greatness. He and his wife have children, and he passes as "an ordinarily successful white man who has made a little money." He's mildly happy. But when his wife dies, he ends his *Autobiography* his way:

My love for my children makes me glad that I am what I am and keeps me from desiring to be otherwise; and yet, when I sometimes open a little box in which I still keep my fast yellowing manuscripts, the only tangible remnants of a vanished dream, a dead ambition, a sacrificed talent, I cannot repress the thought that, after all, I have chosen the lesser part, that I have sold my birthright for a mess of pottage.

Writing (the narrator's writing and Johnson's writing) is the natural container for such fortunate ambivalence. Most of the black men and women he encounters have no market for their birthright.

———

"Chicago, Sunday, Oct. 10. Dear Ma": Langston Hughes's brief story "Passing" is another work of art passing as a familiar letter, casually enveloping large ideas in a small form. Last night a son saw his mother on the street, and today he writes to her. "I felt like a dog, passing you downtown last night and not speaking to you," he says. "You were great, though. Didn't give me a sign that you even knew me, let alone I was your son." He's light-skinned, she's dark; he has a white-collar job, she and his siblings are working-class; he has been to college, they haven't. He has a white girlfriend, he imagines traveling, he can be merely amused by his coworker's racism. He passes. His privilege salts the wounds made by his ordinary adolescent insensitivity. And this is the life his mother wanted for him.

This irony is pointed enough, but the last lines of Hughes's story give the knife of that irony a final turn. "I'm glad there's nothing to stop letters from crossing the color-line," it reads. "Even if we can't meet often, we can write, can't we, Ma?" What

might in another context seem praise of writing's power to transcend differences and speak to a common humanity is revealed
as cruelly self-congratulatory. It allows the boy to deceive himself into thinking he and his mother share more than they do.
And here I am, a white man reading a fictional letter written to a
black woman: I do what she has done. Hughes has gathered us
together to read the same letter. In abstracting away from particulars, writing allows me to participate in anyone's story, allows me
to think I'm kin to any writer, any reader. I can think I've crossed
the color line, and put myself in the place of this black mother.
The knife of Hughes's irony turns outward toward me, too.

I was saying that thoughts of unlived lives are prompted with special force by our families and especially by parents, children, and
siblings. Our bodies seem to be telling us that we're not merely
ourselves but instead ourselves and someone else at the same
time. Entering a family, we've escaped singularity somehow and
become two. In this, a family is more powerful than marriage.
For all the Bible's insistence, and for all the love songs you've
heard, marriage doesn't *really* make one person out of the two of
you. It's only a metaphor. But children—the children we have,
once had, never had—remind us that the difference between the
metaphorical and the literal isn't always clear.

Veracruz

GEORGE STANLEY

In Veracruz, city of breezes & sailors & loud birds,
an old man, I walked the Malecón by the sea,

and I thought of my father, who when a young man
had walked the Malecón in Havana, dreaming of Brazil,

and I wished he had gone to Brazil
& learned magic,

and I wished my father had come back to San Francisco
armed with Brazilian magic, & that he had married
not my mother, but her brother, whom he truly loved.

I wish my father had, like Tiresias, changed himself into
   a woman,
& that he had been impregnated by my uncle, & given
   birth to me as a girl.

I wish that I had grown up in San Francisco as a girl,
a tall, serious girl,

& that eventually I had come to Veracruz,
& walking on the Malecón, I had met a sailor,
a Mexican sailor or a sailor from some other country—
maybe a Brazilian sailor,
& that he had married me, & I had become pregnant
by him,
so that I could give birth at last to my son—the boy
I love.

What magic of generation and re-creation, betrothal and impreg-
nation, gendering and regendering, has formed this family of
phrases? The poet has sighted his ports of call and while traveling
on he has traveled back, Malecón leading to Malecón, Brazil to
Brazil, sending us through a series of variations—Veracruz Havana Brazil San Francisco; old man young man father mother

uncle brother daughter son—so that while everything is what it is in this poem, everything also could have been different, even *this* different: that this man could have mothered his son, the boy he loves. The speaker wishes not to become someone else but to have been someone else and thus to be, now, someone else. All the speaker is, is this person with spectacular capacities for the expression of the desire to be who he is not.

It's true that he regrets opportunities unrealized and paths untaken; he carries them with him as he walks by the sea. But when I read "Veracruz," what I feel most isn't melancholy, but renewing surprise. I travel from word to word and don't know where I'm going, what lies around this line break or after that comma, across this dash or beyond that period. I dip and swerve, like a seabird. The most delightful of these surprises, because the most gently detailed, is the speaker's wish to have grown up in San Francisco not merely as a "girl," but as "a tall, serious girl." After all the aerial extravagance of the speaker's wishes, he alights suddenly, briefly, on this modest image, resting on its own quiet line.

In Havana, the speaker's father dreamt of Brazil, but he didn't enter his dreams and didn't learn the magic of that place. Here, now, in Mexico, the speaker has found his own magic and speaks his own incantations. He's a queer and loving god. His magical capacity for elating revelation takes us so far that by the poem's end the whirlwind of words, the enchainment of the ampersands, the enjambment and paragraphing, seem to have given birth to a child. Stanley doesn't write, "so that I could give birth at last to my son—the boy / I *would have* loved." He writes "the boy / I *love*." The loved boy actually exists, now; he's no ghostly figure or missed opportunity lost in a vaporous, unreal world. What Baudelaire said of poets is true of this speaker: he enjoys the incomparable privilege of being both himself and someone else as he wishes.

————

My older child looks like me and sometimes behaves like me. Both of us have this way of lowering our heavy eyebrows when irritated, the same way of walking when rushed, the same paths of retreat when anxious. We're two separate people, yet they and I share so much. The same is as true for my son as for his sibling: some of my traits live in him, and his in me. It's true, too, of their older sister who died as she was born. How to explain? Unless simply saying "they're my children" is explanation enough.

————

Nowhere does the imagination of other lives throw language into crisis more powerfully than when we're with children. My children: are they some of me or none of me? It's a question for fathers but more intensely one for biological mothers, who have been two or one, two and one, during pregnancy. For nine months and more, the metaphysical and the bodily have been nauseatingly, ecstatically, tediously brought together. This is true for mothers who have given birth, for mothers who have miscarried, for mothers who have given birth to stillborn children, for mothers who have had abortions.

In this poem by Gwendolyn Brooks, such metaphysical issues come to earth with a force scarcely managed:

the mother

Abortions will not let you forget.
You remember the children you got that you did not get,
The damp small pulps with a little or with no hair,

The singers and workers that never handled the air.
You will never neglect or beat
Them, or silence or buy with a sweet.
You will never wind up the sucking-thumb
Or scuttle off ghosts that come.
You will never leave them, controlling your luscious sigh,
Return for a snack of them, with gobbling mother-eye.

I have heard in the voices of the wind the voices of my
    dim killed children.
I have contracted. I have eased
My dim dears at the breasts they could never suck.
I have said, Sweets, if I sinned, if I seized
Your luck
And your lives from your unfinished reach,
If I stole your births and your names,
Your straight baby tears and your games,
Your stilted or lovely loves, your tumults, your mar-
    riages, aches, and your deaths,
If I poisoned the beginnings of your breaths,
Believe that even in my deliberateness I was not
    deliberate.
Though why should I whine,
Whine that the crime was other than mine?—
Since anyhow you are dead.
Or rather, or instead,
You were never made.
But that too, I am afraid,
Is faulty: oh, what shall I say, how is the truth to be said?
You were born, you had body, you died.
It is just that you never giggled or planned or cried.

Believe me, I loved you all.
Believe me, I knew you, though faintly, and I loved, I
    loved you
All.

Who or what are these children that the speaker has not had? What sort of reality do they have, have they had? Are they dead or were they never made? How is the truth to be said? The paradoxes of abortions evacuate Brooks's language. To say, "You were born, you had body, you died" tells us everything and nothing. The command of Brooks's voice gives her helplessness authority: even she is at a loss before her past.

"Believe me, I loved you all. / Believe me, I knew you, though faintly, and I loved, I loved you / All." Here, at the poem's end, the mother speaks from her experience. But at the poem's start, she speaks not of "me" but of "you": "Abortions will never let *you* forget." She generalizes her experience: there are many like her, unable to forget abortions. Before she emerges as an individual, as "I," she's part of a group. And that group, unnervingly, seems to include the reader in its "you." (Me? No matter what my experience, no matter what my gender? How can I measure my distance?) When this "you" then slides around to point at the children who were born, had body, and died, the play of individual and group becomes more unnerving and painful still. Uniqueness is what we share, and we share it even with those of us who were born, had body, and died, who never giggled or planned or cried.

The voices of Brooks's children come to her on the wind, present to her but partial, bodiless. In Molly Peacock's poem "The

Choice," the speaker's past pregnancy returns as a "large / amorphous vapor." This spirit has come to help the speaker, but finds help hard to give—another visiting divinity bringing a balked love.

The Choice

The ghost of my pregnancy, a large
amorphous vapor, much larger than me,
comes when I am alarmed to comfort me,
though it, too, alarms me, and I dodge

away, saying "leave me alone," and the ghost,
always beneficent, says, "You're a tough one
to do things for." The ghost must have done
this lots, it so competently knows I'm lost

and empty. It returns the fullness and slow
connection to all the world just as it is.
When I let it surround me, the embrace is
more mother than baby. How often we don't know

the difference. It's not a dead little thing
without a spinal cord yet, but a spirit of
the parent we all ought to have had, of
possibility. "I was meant to be dead." Thinking

why it said it was *meant* to be dead brings
the tangible comfort: how I used the foetus
shamelessly, how the brief pregnancy showed us,
its father and me, these choices, not shriveling

but choice alive with choice, alive with what's not
taken, or taken up, both pulsing with direction,

for some mistakes are re-takes, or correction,
past times that were forsaken now held when caught.

Again, it's hard to understand the reality of these children you
got that you did not get, who are also somehow these parents you
ought to have had but did not have. The speaker is bewildered by
what we are. And yet, somehow, the embrace of this amorphous
spirit returns her to the fullness of the world, just as it is. She returns to the life she's witnessed, the life she's chosen, "alive with
choice, with what's not/taken, or taken up, both pulsing."

———

"You could not come and yet you go," writes Elizabeth Jennings
to her stillborn child. How is the truth to be said? How are
children who have not lived connected to the world just as it is?
In our confusion, we make metaphors. These children are voices
in the wind, vaporous ghosts. I've seen gravestones that read
"Born Asleep."

———

To tell the story of her marriage and divorce—a story of being
once one and now not one—Sharon Olds uses the conditional
voice. *Stag's Leap* is a story of what might have been. But in the
title of "To Our Miscarried One, Age Thirty Now," where one
might expect Olds to use the conditional—"To Our Miscarried
One, Who Would Be Age Thirty Now," perhaps—she uses no
verb at all. Still, in her clean pentameter line the miscarried one
lives somehow, somewhere, now. "To Our Miscarried One, Age
Thirty Now."

"One" is the least of pronouns: not nothing, but not much of
anything, either. It's the proper name of almost nothing. Olds

knows little about their miscarried one: she knows not whether one is a boy or girl, blond or brunette, quick, fair or funny. Adjectives, remarks Anne Carson, "are in charge of attaching everything in the world to its place in particularity. They are the latches of being." But one is unattached to the world, unlatched, a cloud, an amorphous vapor, not even a voice on the wind. And so even in the word "one" there's loss. "One" also is a number, of course. The question of how to count the ones not living in this world is an old one. In Wordsworth's "We Are Seven," a little maid perplexes the poet by insisting that she has six siblings, though two of them "are in the church-yard laid."

Here's how Olds's poem begins:

> Though I never saw you, only your clouds,
> I was afraid of you, of how you differed
> from what we had wanted you to be. And it's as if
> you waited, then, where such waiting is done,
> for when I would look beside me—and here
> you are, in the world of forms, where my wifehood
> is now, and every action with him,
> as if a thousand years from now
> you and I are in some antechamber
> where the difference between us is of little matter.

To understand their miscarried one, to understand what matters and what matter is, Olds makes comparisons and notes differences. Here, in what she calls a world of forms, the difference between "you and I" is slight, as is (shockingly) the difference between "you" and "what we had wanted you to be." What is this place, this world of forms, where the difference between a miscarried child and what parents want that child to be is not fearsome? A place, evidently, for things that are no longer, things of the past, recollected in comparative tranquility: Olds's wife-hood, her actions with her husband, their miscarried one. A place of memories lifted up and away from things as they are now, a place of abstractions without matter. A place, too, of poetry, that substanceless world of forms. It's a place, evidently, of conjuring magic, for while Olds's sentence starts in the conditional—it's "as if" one waited—it ends with a surprised and surprising indicative:

> —and here
> you are

In this world of forms, Olds needs merely to indicate, merely to point as if with her finger. She's startled, thrown into relief by the sudden transport of one from "as if" to "are." To feel such relief, she must have felt very lonely. It is as if she discovered she had been lonely, lonely for this one, and that loneliness was only ap-parent to her after her husband left.

"I never saw you, only your clouds," the speaker has said. But, then, she looks and sees. She levers herself into vision by a com-parison of losses, and it's brutal:

> That he left me is not much, compared to your leaving the
>   earth—your shifting places
> on it, and shifting shapes—you threw off your
> working clothes of arms and legs, and moved house, from
>   uterus
> to toilet bowl and jointed stem
> and sewer out to float the rivers and
> bays in painless pieces.

As in "Pain I Did Not," where Olds imagined her husband being born out of their marriage, Olds forces herself to look at a bloody, body-felt image. But then, again, she recoils into abstraction. One's body gives way again to the idea of you, mattering without matter:

> the idea of you has come back to where
> I could see you today as a small impromptu
> god of the partial.

This diminished god, a god not whole, but toward whom one is partial, presides over unfinished, incomplete things, like Olds's marriage, and offers her company in her new solitude. Unlike others we've seen, this impromptu god can do something—or so Olds hopes:

> When I leave for good,
> would you hold me in your blue mitt
> for the departure hence. I never thought
> to see you again, I never thought to seek you.

"I never thought / to see you" seems straightforward, but then Olds adds a letter and its halting balance shifts. "I never thought to seek you." Even as she writes, Olds feels the need to return, to repair, to kiss her neglected child, to offer with this poem a prayer to her small god: to atone.

———

A child, part of me and not part of me, departs and returns. A god departs and returns. A. R. Ammons's "Easter Morning" opens this way:

I have a life that did not become,
that turned aside and stopped,
astonished:
I hold it in me like a pregnancy or
as on my lap a child
not to grow old but dwell on

it is to his grave I most
frequently return and return
to ask what is wrong, what was
wrong, to see it all by
the light of a different necessity
but the grave will not heal
and the child,
stirring, must share my grave
with me, an old man having
gotten by on what was left

The controlled and lucid rhythm of the diminishing, end-stopped opening lines soon ripples over a rocky inversion: where you might expect something like, "I hold it in me like a pregnancy or / like a child upon my lap," Ammons writes, "I hold it in me like a pregnancy or / as on my lap a child." The mild puzzlement increases at the end of the stanza, with its slant distinction between growing old and dwelling on. Whose life is this, this life that does not grow old but dwells on, that is perhaps within the speaker like an unborn child and perhaps on his lap as an infant, in an unhealed grave now but to share the speaker's grave in the future? Is this the speaker's life or someone else's?

We're told that the man has returned to his "home country" where "it's convenient to visit / everybody," aunts and uncles, mother, father, and others, too—convenient because these relatives are

> all in the graveyard
> assembled, done for, the world they
> used to wield, have trouble and joy
> in, gone

In this graveyard, then, the man stands. Past and present fold together outside of him and inside of him, for his family, there in the ground, is also "close, close as burrowing under skin"—just as the child within him that could not become also stands outside of him, "by the road / where the mishap occurred, crying out for / help."

It's a quaint, Hardy-esque word, "mishap," a mild word for an event that has left the speaker undone, left everyone undone.

> now
> we all buy the bitter
> incompletions, pick up the knots of
> horror, silently raving, and go on
> crashing into empty ends not
> completions, not rondures the fullness
> has come into and spent itself from

The angularities of "Easter Morning," the roughness and the inversions, the confusions: they voice the bitter incompletion, the empty ends, the knots of horror. They voice what it is to go on, to survive—to survive your childhood, to survive others. Ammons's lines are not a poetic rondure, not full, not perfection. They are, as we are, remains.

I stand on the stump
of a child, whether myself
or my little brother who died, and
yell as far as I can, I cannot leave this place, for
for me it is the dearest and the worst,
it is life nearest to life which is
life lost.

"Art is the nearest thing to life," George Eliot wrote. Yes, and
sometimes that art "is the dearest and the worst, / it is life nearest
to life which is / life lost." I hold that life here, on my lap, I see it
here, in this churchyard, I feel it inside me and outside of me, immeasurably close, immeasurably far.

it is my place where
I must stand and fail

After these rough and torn feelings, the speaker turns toward
his conclusion. It's Easter morning, he says, as if awakening. "A
picture-book, letter-perfect / Easter morning." He's been for a walk
by a brook, listening to birds "lively / with voice." Above him in the
daylight he sees something he's never seen before, "two great
birds / maybe eagles" flying together in poetic patterns. They're
riding the steady air beneath them, then veering, parting, coasting,
circling, rising, rejoining, resting, and finally breaking across the
horizon of trees. Ammons ends "Easter Morning" this way:

it was a sight of bountiful
majesty and integrity: the having
patterns and routes, breaking

from them to explore other patterns or
better ways to routes, and then the
return: a dance sacred as the sap in
the trees, permanent in its descriptions
as the ripples round the brook's
ripplestone: fresh as this particular
flood of burn breaking across us now
from the sun.

Permanent in its descriptions, nature redeems our partial, in-complete, transient life. Sometimes I think that this poem gives the beauty of unlived lives its greatest dignity. It salutes the spirit of resurrection and finds that spirit in the intimate intensity of everyday experience, without relinquishing "the child in me that could not become / was not ready for others to go."

———

It might seem that sibling relations don't accord with all I've been saying, and they don't exactly. For older siblings, the arrival of a brother or sister may seem a fork in the road. But for those later arrivals, older siblings simply are. They're more like large features of your landscape than forks in your road. And yet, as "Easter Morning" intimates, any sibling can intensify the experience of shared exclusion. The existence of a sibling, writes the psychia-trist Juliet Mitchell, forces the realization "that one is not unique, that someone stands exactly in the same place as oneself." Al-though Ammons and his brother are two people, they seem to occupy one body, one grave, one stump: one place, dearest and worst. They are, as Mitchell would say, "alike in position and dif-ferent in identity."

In writing about the death of his brother, Ammons generalizes his experience: "*we all* buy the bitter / incompletions." One task of lyric poetry is to generalize particular experience without betraying it, to move from "I" and "me" and "my brother" to "we" and "us" without sacrificing singularity. Poets are virtuosi of singular and plural. Siblings offer an early education in this characteristically lyric difficulty of modulating between the particular and the general, the solitary and the commonplace. Although I know that I am exactly, only, entirely, here, suddenly there is this other person who is somehow here too. "The sibling," Mitchell writes, "is par excellence someone who threatens the subject's uniqueness." It can be exhilarating and obliterating. "The ecstasy of loving one who is like oneself is experienced at the same time as the trauma of being annihilated by one who stands in one's place." Mitchell's language sounds extreme. But sibling relations *are* extreme, mortal: one can be annihilated by the arrival of a sister, a brother. The very existence of a sibling, Mitchell writes, is "experienced as a *death* of the subject's self."

But one isn't annihilated; one survives. And so a brother, a sister, a sibling teaches that, too—teaches what it is to survive death, to stand on the stump of a child.

––––––––

Though we are two people, we are in one place. Mitchell's metaphor of place is natural and confusing. Like any comparison, it isn't perfect and wouldn't work if it were. It speaks to two aspects of being a person, the aspect of exclusive uniqueness and the aspect of commonness—being exceptional and being anybody. Ammons's names for this place include grave and graveyard. He stands above a grave and lies in it, too. Another name Ammons gives this space is lap. He holds his brother in him as if pregnant.

His brother, who has died, is inside of his body and outside it. I usually think of my body as exclusively mine. But even it is evidently a place that others enter and leave. Our pronouns know this; they're roomy places of ambiguity. In Frank Bidart's elegy "For the AIDS Dead" he says, "You / means I, one, you, as well as the you // inside you constantly talk to."

I don't mean to be trivial or clever, and I don't mean to claim authority in matters not my own. I'm trying to describe how poets, under often anguishing pressures, record our bewilderment at the facts of our embodied identity, facts that complicate the beginning and end of our lives, pregnancy and grave, and so complicate all the time in between. I'm trying to be faithful to their faith that language is an adequate medium through which to experience this bewilderment.

But thinking about language can be a haven from what it describes: we aestheticize our pain and the pain of others. Poetry can acknowledge that, too. Here's Bidart's poem in its entirety:

For the AIDS Dead

FRANK BIDART

The plague you have thus far survived. They didn't.
Nothing that they did in bed that you didn't.

Writing a poem, I cleave to "you." You
means I, one, you, as well as the you

inside you constantly talk to. Without
justice or logic, without

sense, you survived. They didn't.
Nothing that they did in bed that you didn't

"Cleave" separates and clings. It holds together and apart I, one, the you outside and inside. It holds together and apart these things and the words that represent them, "you" and "'you.'" You were in the same place, doing the same things, yet "you survived. They didn't," and you don't, I don't, know why.

———

Early on, I made a show of saying that our singularity is distinct from our mortality, with its own distinct thoughts, distinct emotions. But of course, they're related. Thoughts of death intensify thoughts of your singularity. The more immediately you feel your life will end in the future, the more likely you are in the present to think about the lives you've not led in the past. But these stories of lives unled dwell more on the death of others than on your own. They dwell on what it is to survive others, not to die, but to live on.

———

Hardy's elegies for his wife are faithful to his first chilly passion for her. In "The Going," her death is presented as a turning point of which he was unaware, for he wasn't with her when it happened.

> I
> Saw morning harden upon the wall,
> Unmoved, unknowing
> That your great going
> Had place that moment, and altered all.

This all-altering, unrecognized moment is the empty-armed consummation of a marriage of missed opportunities, for the couple had long been estranged. Even the event of her departure is missing, unverbed in the poem as in his memory: Hardy doesn't write that "your great going / Had *taken* place" but that "your great going / Had place that moment." (The poems Hardy hasn't written can be heard in the ones he has.) An epicure of deprivation, Hardy shows his devotion not by recalling the times they were together but the times they were not, the walk he took without her, the drive she took without him; his poems grieve an intimacy lost, never found, yet somehow lost once more.

This may seem an esoteric grief. But think of the death of an estranged friend, or of a parent who has suffered from dementia. Something happened, and you lost her; now you lose her again. To understand this sort of loss, Hardy returns to paths untaken together.

The Walk

You did not walk with me
Of late to the hill-top tree
    By the gated ways,
    As in earlier days;
    You were weak and lame,
    So you never came,
And I went alone, and I did not mind,
Not thinking of you as left behind.

I walked up there to-day
Just in the former way:
    Surveyed around
    The familiar ground
    By myself again:
    What difference, then?

Only that underlying sense
Of the look of a room on returning thence.

Reading the poem aloud you feel the pull and hobbled haul of
its rhythm. The easy iambic movement of the opening words
carries you over the line break and through "of late," and then
sends you up the skipping, alliteration of "to the hill-top tree";
the memory of the inner rhyme between "late" and "gated" lingers into the quick end rhyme assonance of "ways" and "days."
By the time you've swung past the peculiar column of couplets
in the middle of the stanza, your gait has become uncertain,
off-balance.

You did not walk with me
Of late to the hill-top tree
   By the gated ways,
   As in earlier days;
   You were weak and lame,
   So you never came,
And I went alone, and I did not mind,
Not thinking of you as left behind.

Reading the last line of the stanza, you're led to pause after "Not
thinking of you" so that, for a passing moment, the poet walks
along, not minding or thinking of his wife at all—before you learn
that, no, he was not thinking of her *as left behind*. In the same
way, if you pause at the end of the poem's first line, you find yourself momentarily thinking that the poet's wife did not walk with
him at all—before you learn that she did not walk with him *of
late*. Qualification, second thoughts, return and revision: the
smallest movement of your thought recapitulates Hardy's largest

preoccupations. His wife has died, and he reconsiders his marriage. And he reconsiders it in one particular way: he doesn't ask if his wife shared his feelings, or if they were well matched or happy together. He asks: what did I miss?

Of late, he left her behind; now she's left him behind. He walked alone in the past; now he walks alone again. "What difference, then?" The couplets of the second stanza raise this final question and force a pause before you confront the answer:

> Only that underlying sense
> Of the look of a room on returning thence.

In these lines, Hardy doesn't mention the woman, his wife of thirty-eight years, who has died—doesn't say, for instance,

> Only that underlying sense
> Of the loss of her on returning thence

He doesn't say "the look of *our* room on returning thence," or "the look of *her* room." Hardy says, "the look of *a* room." He has pulled away from the particular room in which they lived together, and generalized it into any room, a room like one you or I would know. And so, we're invited in. But only so far, and as we enter, Hardy slips out. Generalizing his experience, he makes it impersonal. Such is Hardy's unobtrusive virtuosity that the choice of a single article—"a," the word that means maybe the least of all words—makes all the difference.

When I seek others to discover who I am, where do I find them? Do I look to my friends? My colleagues? My parents, partner, children? Family members? The dead? How far afield do I go to make my measurements?

Virginia Woolf has an essay, one of her most famous, called "The Death of a Moth"—an elegy five paragraphs long. In it she handles with the lightest of touches both fragile particulars and weighty abstractions: a moth and death on a September morning. She sees the moth on a windowpane as she sits in her study; beyond the glass lie the fields of Sussex. It's the moth's energy, "the same energy which inspired the rooks, the ploughmen, the horses, and even, it seemed, the lean bare-backed downs," that draws Woolf's attention. The moth is one with all she sees beyond the windowpane. "Watching him, it seemed as if a fibre, very thin but pure, of the enormous energy of the world had been thrust into his frail and diminutive body. As he often crossed the pane, I could fancy that a thread of vital light became visible. He was little or nothing but life."

The moth flutters then falls, tries to rise and falls again, dropping to the sill.

> It flashed on me that he was in difficulties; he could no longer raise himself; his legs struggled vainly. But, as I stretched out a pencil, meaning to help him to right himself, it came over me that the failure and the awkwardness were the approach of death. I laid the pencil down again.

Woolf looks out through the window and across the fields, now quiet. It's midday and work has stopped; the birds have flown to feed in the brooks.

> The horses stood still. Yet the power was there all the same, massed outside indifferent, impersonal, not attending to

anything in particular. Somehow it was opposed to the little hay-coloured moth. It was useless to try to do anything. One could only watch the extraordinary efforts made by those tiny little legs against an oncoming doom, which could, had it chosen, have submerged an entire city, not merely a city, but masses of human beings; nothing, I knew, had any chance against death.

Woolf looks on helplessly at the struggle of one thin thread of life, the world's enormous energy compressed in one frail body. She is an impotent guardian angel, an eloquent recording angel. "The thought of all that life might have been had he been born in any other shape caused one to view his simple activities with a kind of pity." And yet his fate is no different from hers, from yours, from ours.

Atonement

She will never be an artist: she has no notion of being
anybody but herself.

—GEORGE ELIOT, *DANIEL DERONDA*

God probably preferred to speak of His world in the subjunctive
of potentiality . . . for God makes the world and while doing so
thinks that it could just as easily be some other way

—ROBERT MUSIL, *THE MAN WITHOUT QUALITIES*

There is no assignable end to the depth of us to which language
reaches; . . . nevertheless there is no end to our separateness.
We are endlessly separate for no reason. But then we are
answerable for everything that comes between us; if not
for causing it then for continuing it; if not for denying
it then for affirming it; if not for it then to it.

—STANLEY CAVELL, *THE CLAIM OF REASON*

I can know neither all that words reveal, nor all that they con-
ceal. Which is to say, I can't know fully how answerable I am for
words, to words.

The first half of Ian McEwan's *Atonement* takes place at the
Surrey estate of Jack and Emily Tallis on a June weekend in 1935.
A family party gathers, drawing together Emily, her daughters
Cecilia and Briony, and her son Leon; her twin nephews Pierrot
and Jackson and their older sister Lola; Leon's wealthy London
friend Paul Marshall; and Robbie Turner, the son of the estate
gardener, whom the Tallises have helped to raise. Across the
course of the weekend, Cecilia and Robbie, both fresh from university, fall in love and enact a drama eagerly observed by Briony,

who, at thirteen, thinks of herself as an author. Cecilia and Robbie are in the summer lull between childhood and adulthood; their motionless days hum with possibility. It's a time and place for flirtation—for its excitement and its anxieties and its strange, swelling suspension of time. The world lies all before them: Where to choose? What paths has university opened for Cecilia? Where will she live? Whom will she marry? Every moment seems to press possibilities upon her: what will she wear, eat, do, say? Before Paul Marshall arrives, she wonders, "as she sometimes did when she met a man for the first time, if this was the one she was going to marry, and whether it was this particular moment she would remember for the rest of her life—with gratitude, or profound and particular regret." And Robbie, having won his first at university, what should he do? What career should he follow? Schoolmaster? University don? Writer? Doctor? Evening comes, and time slows to stillness. What is said of Robbie is true of Cecilia as well: he possesses a hoard of time, "the luxury of an unspent fortune. He had never before felt so self-conscious young, nor experienced such appetite, such impatience for the story to begin." Everything simmers and shakes.

But all these possibilities are abruptly canceled. In the afternoon, Briony has seen Cecilia take off her clothes in Robbie's presence in order to retrieve the broken pieces of a vase dropped into a fountain; later, Briony reads a note from Robbie in which he declares his newfound desire for Cecilia; later still, she interrupts the two of them having hurried sex in the house library. When, at the end of the day, in dark and uncertain circumstances, her cousin Lola is raped, Briony identifies Robbie as the rapist.

The plot of the second section of the novel, then, lays out the grim consequences of this event. Robbie has spent five years in prison and has been discharged into the infantry; it's 1940, and he's retreating toward Dunkirk. As we read, details heap up with the bodies: strafing attacks scatter civilians in flight; a crater replaces a woman and her child; a bomb blast lifts and drives Robbie into the ground, filling his mouth with dirt. While he marches, Cecilia, having left her family in appalled outrage at their enthusiasm for his prosecution, serves as a nurse in London, where Briony is a nurse-in-training. The descriptions of nursing are as bloody as those of the war, and the rhythms of hospital life—the waiting thoughts and the frantic work when thought is impossible—are as insistent as those of wartime.

Throughout these events, the characters of the novel are presented as elaborately singular, with rich and distinctive inner experiences. Early in the novel the precocious Briony has a moment of weighty reflection:

Was being Cecilia just as vivid an affair as being Briony? Did her sister also have a real self concealed behind a breaking wave, and did she spend time thinking about it, with a finger held up to her face? Did everybody . . . ? If the answer was yes, then the world, the social world, was unbearably complicated, with two billion voices, and everyone's thoughts striving in equal importance and everyone's claim on life as intense, and every one thinking they were unique, when no one was. One could drown in irrelevance. But if the answer was no, then Briony was surrounded by machines, intelligent and pleasant enough on the outside, but lacking the bright and private *inside* feeling she had.

The questions Briony asks aren't answered by the novel, exactly, but dramatized. Robbie's experience of battle forces his intimate separation upon him with desperate clarity. Here's the first image we have from the war:

> A leg in a tree. A mature plane tree, only just in leaf. The leg was twenty feet up, wedged in the first forking of the trunk, bare, severed cleanly above the knee. . . . There was no sign of blood or torn flesh. It was a perfect leg, pale, smooth, small enough to be a child's. The way it was angled in the fork, it seemed to be on display, for their benefit or enlightenment: this is a leg.

A moment later, Robbie comes across "a man and his collie dog walking behind a horse-drawn plough," unaware of the convoy passing him. It seemed to Robbie to be

> like the deadly pursuit of a hunt to hounds, while over the next hedge a woman in the back seat of a passing motor car was absorbed in her knitting, and in the bare gardens of a new house a man was teaching his son to kick a ball. Yes, the ploughing would still go on and there'd be a crop, someone to reap it and mill it, others to eat it, and not everyone would be dead.

All the characters are singular, separate. But they understand themselves, and we understand them, by comparison.

Having appraised her appearance in her mirror, Cecilia takes off her black crepe de chine dress, dissatisfied. She reconsiders her options, chooses a neat moiré silk number, and slips it on. She looks at herself again and again takes it off. Finally, she chooses the dress she knew she wanted to wear all along: a new green gown, backless. Dressed and redressed, perfumed and ornamented, she now looks not at herself in the mirror but out her door—only, startlingly, to see someone else looking back at her. One of the twins stands before her in tears, unable to find proper clothes for dinner in this strange house. Meanwhile, Robbie sits at his typewriter in his study, planning to write his note to Cecilia. He considers the tone to take. Proper or jokey? Melodramatic or plaintive? In draft after draft he worries about how he'll look. After a moment of reverie, he writes, "In my dreams I kiss your cunt, your sweet wet cunt. In my thoughts I make love to you all day long." That won't do. He checks his watch and realizes he needs to hurry. He pulls out a new sheet, writes a new note in longhand, finishes dressing, speaks with his mother, grabs the note, and goes out. Rather than give it to Cecilia himself, he asks Briony to pass the note along, and contentedly watches her disappear through the softening light before realizing that he's given her the wrong draft. Robbie and Cecilia live in parallel: they consider how to present themselves in public, to each other; they test out different possibilities; and as they contrive their futures, others—the world in the form of younger children—interrupt them to unhappy effect.

Like Briony concealed behind a breaking wave, Robbie and Cecilia are each enclosed and driven to overcome that enclosure, to open up to each other. The sex between them is pointedly penetrative: "Daringly they touched the tips of their tongues . . . [which were] alive and slippery muscle[s], moist flesh on flesh. . . . She bit him on the cheek, not quite playfully . . . [before her] membrane parted." Briony's later work as a nurse is rendered, with unsettling but sure similarities, as a matter of repairing bodies battle has opened:

> Using a pair of surgical tongs, she began carefully pulling
> away the sodden, congealed lengths of ribbon gauze from

the cavity in the side of his face. When the last was out, the resemblance to the cut-away model they used in anatomy class was only faint. This was all ruin, crimson and raw. She could see through his missing cheek to his upper and lower molars, and the tongue glistening, and hideously long. Further up, where she hardly dared look, were the exposed muscles around his eye socket. So intimate, and never intended to be seen.

In love and war, these people are concealed and revealed, held apart and joined together. As we read, we pace off the distance between them—between their bodies, between their thoughts. Cecilia thinks that she has mended the broken vase so perfectly that no one would know that it had been broken. But she doesn't know that Briony saw the accident from one of the nursery's wide-open windows—nor does Briony know that we saw her, as it were, from a window yet more distant. (Something priceless has been broken; someone has secretly tried to restore it to its original wholeness; and someone else has watched the whole process: we'll learn that this is an allegory for the novel itself.)

Singular individuals, decisive events, forking roads: with these in place, the characters live in the aftermath of that June day in 1935, consigned to the unhappy company of the people they are not. Like Briony, who worries that "her life was going to be lived in one room, without a door," they all long "to have someone else's past, to be someone else." As the novel moves toward its conclusion, the crush of all they are not only intensifies. Briony makes her way across the city to visit Cecilia, looking to find a way to undo what she has done. She's come to realize that she was mistaken about Robbie and wants to recant. She now believes that Paul Marshall was the rapist. But as she walks through South London, she senses that she has another self, no less real, who has chosen not to visit Cecilia but to walk back toward the hospital. Which is the real and which the imagined person, she wonders. When she then arrives at Cecilia's flat, Briony is surprised to find Robbie there, visiting while on leave. In a tense scene he tells her that if she wants to recant she must start by writing a true account of what happened on that June evening, five years earlier.

But the trick of the novel, or its first trick, lies in the revelation that what we've read is in fact that account, written and rewritten over decades. After Robbie demands that Briony describe what truly happened, Part Three of *Atonement* ends this way:

> She knew what was required of her. Not simply a letter, but a new draft, an atonement, and she was ready to begin.
>
> *BT*
> *London, 1999*

The narrative we've read was written by Briony Tallis, now seventy-seven years old and, we learn, a long-successful novelist. The novel's second trick, then, lies in the revelation on its final page that Robbie actually died at Dunkirk, and Cecilia in a bomb blast at the Balham tube station. After Robbie was taken away from the Tallis estate in the early morning hours, the couple never had a private moment together. Their lives ended and Briony remained, writing.

The weekend party, the rape, the march to Dunkirk, the days of nursing, the bleak trip to Cecilia's flat: these now appear, in retrospect, not as things that have happened but as things that have been written. Everything and nothing changes: the words remain the same, but their meaning shifts entirely. What we unthinkingly took to be the words of an invisible narrator, offstage and easily ignored, suddenly appear to have been written, and written by someone we know. It's as if we've been reading one long dramatic monologue. Before I saw Briony's initials crouched on the page, I was happily unconcerned with why I was being told this story. But when I learn that it's being told not by a third-person narrator but by a character, questions of motivation wheel into view. What exactly has Briony done? And why has she done it? To understand, I need to return to where I've been.

The writing in the first half of *Atonement*, remarks John Updike, is "conspicuously good. . . . *This is written*, each page subliminally announces." Now that I look, I can see that this writtenness has been evident throughout. The clues to Briony's authorship were so thickly strewn on the ground that they must have crackled underfoot as I walked. The fastidious phrases, the crisply articulated voice, the anthology allusions; I wonder that I could have missed them. Each object, each person in this world has been carefully placed under a plate of clean glass. This story has not been written, I think, but curated. Cecilia and her brother Leon have been arguing by the swimming pool:

> There was nothing she could do, nothing she could make Leon do, and she suddenly felt the pointlessness of argument. She lolled against the warm stone, lazily finishing her cigarette and contemplating the scene before her—the foreshortened slab of chlorinated water, the black inner tube of a tractor tyre propped up against a deck chair, the two men in cream linen suits of infinitesimally different hues, bluest-grey smoke rising against the bamboo screen. It looked carved, fixed, and again, she felt it: it had happened a long time ago, and all outcomes, on all

scales—from the tiniest to the most colossal—were already in place. Whatever happened in the future, however superficially strange or shocking, would also have an unsurprising, familiar quality, inviting her to say, but only to herself, Oh yes, of course. That. I should have known.

Adjectives are brushed onto all the nouns—the suits are cream, the smoke bluest-grey, the inner tube black—so that the world seems to come to me as a beguiling work of art. (That the slab is foreshortened is a nice touch: foreshortening brings the world closer and crowds me with its reality.) Like the leg in the tree, it's on display, and for my benefit. And I believed in it—believed that the world might be art and might be meant for me.

But, again, what I took to be the work of a third-person narrator was the work of a character. Description was also expression: the description of what happened in the years following 1935 expressed Briony's view of things in 1999. When she describes Cecilia, standing by the pool and thinking that everything seemed to have "happened a long time ago, and all outcomes, on all scales—from the tiniest to the most colossal—were already in place," Briony is also expressing her own situation in 1999, for of course, it all did happen a long time ago, and all the outcomes, tiny and colossal, are already in place. I thought that these words merely recounted Cecilia's experience in the past, but I now realize that they also convey Briony's state as she writes. A second coat of meaning has been added, the paint thickened: $n + 1$.

This layering of description and expression is everywhere in the novel. Following a minor calamity, the young Briony describes her desire to "go back down the lines of branching consequences to the point before the destruction began. She needed to contemplate with eyes closed the full richness of what she had lost, what she had given away." What is this, but an expression of what the older Briony has done in writing her story as a whole? Or again, a little later, Cecilia reflects that all day long "she had been feeling strange, and seeing strangely, as though everything was already long in the past, made more vivid by posthumous ironies she could not quite grasp." Indeed. Everything is long in the past, the ironies are posthumous, and neither Cecilia in 1935 nor Briony in 1999 can quite grasp them. Once more: in writing, thinks the thirteen-year-old Briony, self-exposure "was inevitable"; describing a character, she will expose herself—as she in fact does, writing here about her young self. (She exposes herself in secret—one description of what it is to write.)

But to say, as Updike does, that the novel is written is to say that it's meant to be read: Briony's tale is conspicuously intended for reading. Materials for interpretation have been duly provided. We have been given not only the author's biography but also the historical context of the book, variant drafts of the final text, and allusions to the literary tradition from which it emerged. We've even been given an improbably long rejection letter from the editor of a press. Robbie and Cecilia both studied literature at Cambridge, and the novel is contrived as if for their well-trained analysis. They were, after all, imagined to be its first readers. Now that they can't turn its pages, we do so in their place.

Cecilia getting dressed and undressed, Robbie writing draft after draft; the scenes of lovemaking and of nursing: the novel is a crisscrossing pattern of paired parallels left for us to find. We compared characters, themes, and settings, the scenes of lovemaking and of nursing, of dressing and drafting. I noticed, with a modest flush of gratification, the echo of Auden, the leg that had fallen through clouds of artillery smoke while the man walked with the horse-drawn plough and the dog. I saw something amazing but didn't turn away. As Updike shrewdly notes, my capacities were flattered—I congratulated myself on my acuity and was pleased that I was up to the task. How unlike everyday life, when everything seems so often to rush past, heedless and unheeded.

We're back at the ideal of reading we first saw in "The God Who Loves You," the ideal of the work as full of meaning. We do what we can to make it so. For if art is unendingly significant, then so might our lives be, for a moment, if we read truly, closely enough. We might have no reason to wish ourselves otherwise. We exercise our ingenuity in justifying what might appear as blemishes or errors, discovering why they might have been intended. We're loving readers.

But now we learn that our experience has been contrived, our bits of clever meaning-making planned. We were in the presence of meaning and thought we possessed it but didn't. The very satisfaction that we took from the novel was only a sign of our naïveté. We've even overlooked our blindness: "*Of course, of course,*" Cecilia thinks when she looks back and realizes she's been in love. "How had she not seen it? Everything was explained. The whole day, the weeks before, her childhood. A lifetime. It was clear to her now." There was more to know, and we could have known it then, but we only know it now. And Briony, whom in fact we've never liked much, has been at the window watching all along. Reviewers of *Atonement* recurrently remark on what "we might have known," what "we might notice" as we read the novel through the first time: yes, we might have. We had the capacity. But did we?

And so we feel hard done by. But perhaps Briony has been treated no better. When she holds her hand before her and meditates on her will, she asks, "Did her sister also have a real self concealed behind a breaking wave, and did she spend time thinking about it, with a finger held up to her face." (*Sic.*) There is no question mark. Did McEwan say to his copyeditor, "No, don't put the question mark in, I intend it that way, with a full stop. It's no mistake of mine, but one of Briony's." Who is to blame for this mistake, if it's a mistake? How can I know? Briony's prose is a slightly elevated version of the style one might expect from McEwan himself. But the difference is so slight that I'm often unsure whose writing I'm reading. Say you notice an occasional heavy-handedness in the novel. Robbie has given the letter to Briony, and we're given a description of him leaning against the parapet, watching "her bobbing and receding form fade into the dusk. It was an awkward age in a girl, he thought contentedly." It's a bit of genre painting, the dusk, the receding form, the man angled in the gloaming. But the word "contentedly"—does it send the description a bit over the top? Is this overwritten? The paint too thick? Say that it is overwritten. By whom? Is this Briony's bad writing or McEwan's? Or again, an earlier chapter has opened this way: "Within the half hour Briony would commit her crime. Conscious that she was sharing the night expanse with a maniac, she kept close to the shadowed walls of the house." Isn't the management of voice here a bit clumsy? It's the aged narrator who knows that Briony will soon "commit her crime," but it's young Briony who, not two lines later, thinks that there's a "maniac" on the loose. Is this lurch a clever hint of Briony's imperfect authorship? Or is it simply sloppiness on McEwan's part? Or again (you see how the obsession can mount), perhaps you remember—or must be reminded, as I was—that Briony herself sees a hovering, disembodied leg a few pages before Robbie sees one. She's walking through the June evening, looking for the twins, and sees "a cylindrical object that seemed to hover" in the air; only slowly does she realize it is her mother's leg, not disembodied at all but obscured and oddly angled. Surely this leg is McEwan's doing, not Briony's. But then you wonder about the later allusion to Auden's "Musée des Beaux Arts" and puzzle over its dating. You make a tick in the margins and look it up: the poem was first printed in 1940, when Robbie was supposed to be marching. Surely he wouldn't have had access to a poem so recently published. Surely, then, we're to think of this not as his thought but as an indulgent flourish by the author. But *which* author? Is McEwan whispering to us, almost inaudibly, that Robbie's story was being written not by him but by the less accomplished Briony? Then it wouldn't be McEwan's intention, but Briony's. Well, which is it?

Down this path a peculiar madness lies. I said that one promise art holds out is that your own life might be worth the sort of attention you pay to art, that I'm now paying to this novel. But how much attention is enough? When do you stop? I know: this isn't everyone's problem, or anyone's problem all the time. ("Stop me before I interpret any more!") But the clockwork contrivance of *Atonement* is designed to encourage it. McEwan leads us to a spot where success and failure are indistinguishable, and so he invites obsession. Perhaps he has fabricated a piece of deliberately flawed prose, has tapped the crystal of his work ever so slightly, so that a crack appears and the lights passing through it are refracted, tinted, just so. Perhaps he has intended imperfection and called it finished.

There must be a name for that ragged border between the bust and the base, the bare feet and the rough stone beneath them. A sculpture now stands before you, complete, yet the chiseled rock it once was remains. Sometimes you can see art emerge from its origins in prose, too. In Woolf's diaries, you hear her trying out sentences for her novels. And in James's prefaces, remember, we saw him ascend playfully into iambic pentameter. "She'll strangle it in the cradle, even as she pretends, all so cheeringly, to rock it; wherefore I'll stay her hand while yet there's time." *Atonement* is written along that border between art and reality, as if to test it, and us. Like Bruegel painting the limits of painting, McEwan writes the limits of writing within his writing. If only I knew where.

Say that he has designed all this, that McEwan's intention pervades every sentence of the book: we've been manipulated and Briony sacrificed so that he can remain flawless. Wherever I go, whatever thoughts I have, he's been there before me, engineering them. I hear the heels of his loafers clacking away ahead of me on a distant marble floor. Naturally I'm resentful. (*Atonement* makes book reviewers and academic critics like me especially annoyed. We've been exposed and fooled, like everyone else. We're anybody, it turns out, and not exceptional. And yet this is our job!) Is such cleverness, such preening forgivable? That he shuffles his cleverness off onto his narrator doesn't get McEwan off the hook. In these moods I say to myself, here's a novel about our capacity to cause exorbitant, irrevocable damage, and its author responds with scurrying cleverness. As if being smart could make up for the pain we have caused. But then I realize how familiar a desire this is, and how often I share it.

Let's return to Briony. What would it be like to craft an intricate, artistic story for an audience that you intend not to appreciate it? To take readers down one road when another was the real one? And then, having contrived their ignorance and their error, to point it out to them? Briony has engineered our stupidity and engineered our knowledge of our stupidity. She has engineered her own knowingness. Why? As I've said, questions of her intentions suddenly wheel into view—or, rather, I realize with another descent of spirit that they've been on view all along. When the flowers that Cecilia arranges in her repaired vase fall into "willful neatness" rather than the "artful disorder" she hoped for, she consoles herself with the thought that the crude and boorish Paul Marshall, for whom they are being arranged, will not notice. I was given another metaphor for the novel, which is nothing if not a display of willful neatness. Am I no more discerning than Paul Marshall?

It's past time to ask, and not only about this novel, *why* do we return to the past to understand who we are now? One of Briony's purposes in drafting and redrafting her novel, clearly enough, is to manage her traumatic guilt, to master the event that has defined her life. She puts it into a story. As a child, we're told, she was "possessed by a desire to have the world just so": all the animals on her model farm faced the same way, toward her. If the world in the years since has played cruelly with her desires, fiction has continued to offer its orderly consolations. Here, at least, "the perfection of the scene" might be achieved.

This is true enough. But Briony has a more urgent motive to write this story: she wants company. As a child, we're told, she wanted to be exceptional, but she's spent her adulthood trying to convince herself that she's anyone. Juliet Mitchell speaks of that moment "when analytic patients—indeed all patients, all of us—come to discover the huge relief of that dreaded fate that we are 'ordinary'; at heart we are just like anyone else, as anyone else is like us." In her desperation, Briony has engineered this likeness. For, like her, I wanted things to be different, wanted the lovers to have gone on living; like her, I wanted a story that fit my desires. I was ready for Cecilia and Robbie to live happily ever after, to have peaceful love after all their suffering. My expectations, shaped by all the stories I've read, blinded me, just as Briony's expectations, shaped by all she had read, blinded her as she peered into the night. I wanted the world to be like art; I made my comparisons, and got it all wrong.

Briony draws us in to join her in her imperfection. But our company is not what she most wants. She wants Cecilia and Robbie. Writing seemed a way to achieve this. Go back one last time to the leg hung on display, that gelid extract from Auden's poem. Listen to the halting movement of Briony's sentences: "A leg in a tree. A mature plane tree, only just in leaf. The leg was twenty feet up, wedged in the first forking of the trunk, bare, severed cleanly above the knee. . . ." From tree to mature plane tree, to mature plane tree just in leaf; from leg to leg twenty feet up, to leg twenty feet up and wedged in the first forking, a bare leg, a bare leg severed, a bare leg severed cleanly. . . . As she describes the things Robbie sees, Briony imagines Robbie's mind moving exactly as hers moves, registering in his thoughts each new feature as she registers them in each new word. The path of his thoughts and the path of her thoughts share a syntax. They become one. The juddering movement of Robbie's eyes and thoughts as he takes in what is before him in France is the movement of Briony's thoughts as she takes in what is before her in her imagination. While she writes, they're together. When she stops, he's lost.

But of course, Briony wasn't present when Robbie saw the leg, if he ever saw a leg. Of course, she doesn't know his thoughts. All her scholarship—she's learned what she can about Dunkirk—won't give her what he saw and heard and smelled and touched. They're separate, and knowledge can't overcome that separation. But she writes as if at some point, with the addition of one more compulsively described detail, Robbie will return from being a character to being a person, will magically change from something that was written to someone who is real, with her, at one. The word "atonement" comes from the idea of being at one: Christ on the cross, suffering the passion of incarnation, takes on our sins and so overcomes our separation. As if being separate were punishment for original sin, from which we are now free. $N+1$ can be an elating possibility. But it's not one that either Briony or McEwan can entertain forever. At some point, writing and reading end.

As his novel comes to its close, McEwan summons the last of the crippled deities who have watched over our progress:

> The problem these fifty-nine years has been this: how can a novelist achieve atonement when, with her absolute power of deciding outcomes, she is also God? There is no one, no entity higher or higher form that she can appeal to, or be reconciled with, that can forgive her. There is nothing outside her. In her imagination she has set the limits and the terms. No atonement for God, or novelists, even if they are atheists.

Imagining another world, Briony has made of herself a paper god, omnipotent over nothing, director and drama queen of an empty stage. Commanding that world, she can't distinguish the possibility of atonement from another possibility, in which she's only one, nor can we as we read. Is our experience solitary or shared? As we read, we inhabit our uncertainty. At one or only one?

CHAPTER THREE

All the Difference

Something nameless opens in the heart.
—JANE HIRSHFIELD, "HISTORY AS THE PAINTER BONNARD"

W e can avoid second thoughts by not starting or by not ending. Any hope of not starting is long gone, and the consolations of not ending have grown stale. It's time to allow this book its imperfection.

———

Let me gather my thoughts. In some moods, being one person seems a limitation: I'm *only* one person. When I'm with others, or perhaps just thinking of them, this singularity can feel like separation: I'm one person *apart* from others. Living is exclusive. And it is irrevocable: I can't retrace my steps. But this is true of us all: we're all traveling down one path among many possibilities, and we can't go back. We're all exceptional and anybody. Of course, we don't dwell on these things all the time, only when we're encouraged. But some experiences encourage us more than others: pursuing a career, marriage, pregnancy, parenting, passing, having a sibling, surviving. Because these experiences are socially and historically shaped, some periods and cultures have prompted thoughts of unled lives more than others. I believe we're in the midst of one such moment now. The waning of the lifelong career, the increased number of women pursuing careers, the spread of birth control, the legalization of abortion, the increased number of surrogate parents and adoptions, an expanded understanding of "emerging adulthood," the legalization of gay marriage, the increased visibility of transgender people, the growing number of adults tending their aging parents, the development of social media and its intensification of social comparison: each of these circumstances and others have changed at different rates, according to different historical logics, but together they have engendered the unled lives crowding us now. When I described my project to a friend, he said, "Ah—YOLO + FOMO."

In this crowd of unreal others, I sometimes imagine replacing the person I am with someone else; sometimes, more modestly, I imagine having some of that person's qualities while remaining myself; sometimes, less modestly, I imagine having both my life and her life. Whichever I imagine—and often it's not clear which I'm imagining—I recognize my separateness and measure the distance between us. Each art makes these measurements in its own way, using its own tools, as the artist attempts to understand what we are.

———

Early on, I said that Frost's "The Road Not Taken" is an extravagant poem, a poem of metaphysical resignation. *Atonement* is certainly true to that extremity: the distant world of prewar

England, the horror of rape, Dunkirk, the elaborately self-deceived child, her glossy, bottomless guilt, and the elaborate ruse of the novel itself. No wonder that the thought of paths untaken desolates Briony. But you can starve from ordinary longing, too. "The Road Not Taken" knows this: it's a mild poem as well as an extravagant one. What does it feel like to live in such mild extremity?

———

When, yesterday, I looked at the softness of the sky, at the differing speeds of the clouds' movement, their infinitely varied molding, at the folds of light that curved around some clouds to flash others upward, my heart softened. (The blue sky arched over the green oak tree and made a nest in its leaves.) My pleasure was immediate and enough. But when, today, I look out on the rain, see that the sky is gray, and feel the chilly air, I think to myself, yesterday's weather was so much better.

Wonder, joy, sorrow, anger, fear, delight, irritation, dismay, heartache, indignation, love . . . these feelings are immediate and pure. They come to me directly, on their own. But regret and relief don't, nor do their cousins rue and wistfulness and lament and gloat and schadenfreude and pity and envy and resentment and, sometimes, pride and exaltation. It may feel as if these emotions enter and spread through me in an instant, but I've created them by comparison.

———

In Dickens's *Great Expectations* we haven't heard three sentences from Pip's sister, Mrs. Joe, before she has rewritten Pip's life and imagined his death: "If it warn't for me you'd have been to the churchyard long ago, and stayed there," she says. It doesn't take much longer for her to rewrite her own life: "Perhaps if I warn't a blacksmith's wife, and (what's the same thing) a slave with her apron never off, I should have been to hear the [Christmas] Carols." Hers is the first of many portraits of people who understand adulthood as a mean trick and others as agents of their entrapment. Mrs. Joe finds her comic double in a woman named Mrs. Pocket, who, we're told, should have married an aristocrat, but didn't. She is married to Mr. Pocket, who should have been an aristocrat but wasn't, and is the mother of seven Pocket children, "the young nobles that ought to have been." Regret is the door through which Mrs. Joe barges into her days, but that same door allows Mrs. Pocket to exit hers, and sail off for her true, titled identity elsewhere.

Having hung his novel with such clouds of regret, Dickens can then let rays of relief break through. Late in the story, after all his expectations have come to nothing, Pip travels back home to see his childhood friend Biddy, intending to ask her to marry him. As he walks along, he imagines what he'll do when he sees her. He drafts a little proposal scene for them to act out:

> [my] purpose was that I would go to Biddy, that I would show her how humbled and repentant I came back, that I would tell her how I had lost all I once hoped for, that I would remind her of our old confidences in my first unhappy time. Then I would say to her, "Biddy. . . ."

But Pip must scrap this carefully crafted, entirely delusional script when he comes upon Biddy and his widowed stepfather, Joe, beaming, just married. Dazed by the contrast between the scene he sketched and the reality in front of him, Pip collapses. When he recovers, his first thought is one of thankfulness: he had often thought of telling Joe that he wanted to marry Biddy but never did. "How irrevocable would have been his knowledge of it!" Like Pip himself, we experience what happens as we experience the rest of the novel, through the lens of what hasn't.

Regret and relief are the emotions we've seen most often in these stories, and regret much more often than relief. Either may be overwhelming, but neither is obscure. Their sources are usually clear. I said something foolish or couldn't help a friend; I remembered a name in time or narrowly missed rear-ending a car. I know what I'm feeling and know why I'm feeling it. Words come easily. But Briony's condition is of a different order from that of someone who wishes she had done differently, harder to know and to voice. To say that she *regrets* what she has done scarcely touches her wretchedness. She's lost a world to live in. Maybe I can put it this way: regret, relief, and their kin arise from within my life; emotions like Briony's arise when I step outside of it. I feel a grief or gratitude that's total and goes all the way down.

"Leading a human life is a full-time occupation," writes Thomas Nagel, "to which everyone devotes decades of intense concern."

This fact is so obvious that it is hard to find it extraordinary and important. Each of us lives his own life—lives with himself twenty-four hours a day. What else is he supposed to do—live someone else's life? Yet humans have the special capacity to step back and survey themselves, and the lives to which they are committed, with

that detached amazement which comes from watching an
ant struggle up a heap of sand. Without developing the il-
lusion that they are able to escape from their highly specific
and idiosyncratic position, they can view it sub specie
aeternitatis—and the view is at once sobering and comical.

Obvious and extraordinary; sobering and comical: Nagel's con-
tradictions confirm my sense that the sources of these queasy feelings are hard for reason to find. They're quicksilver contradictory and inconstant, they wash in waves up my skin. What is it
to be a person?

Here's a pair of poems, one sober and one comical. They're both
fastidiously detailed, ample and exact. Sober first:

I Remember, I Remember

PHILIP LARKIN

Coming up England by a different line
For once, early in the cold new year,
We stopped, and, watching men with number-plates
Sprint down the platform to familiar gates,
"Why, Coventry!" I exclaimed. "I was born here."

I leant far out, and squinnied for a sign
That this was still the town that had been "mine"
So long, but found I wasn't even clear
Which side was which. From where those cycle-crates
Were standing, had we annually departed
For all those family hols? . . . A whistle went:

Things moved. I sat back, staring at my boots.
"Was that," my friend smiled, "where you 'have your
    roots'?"
No, only where my childhood was unspent,
I wanted to retort, just where I started:
By now I've got the whole place clearly charted.
Our garden, first: where I did not invent
Blinding theologies of flowers and fruits,
And wasn't spoken to by an old hat.
And here we have that splendid family
I never ran to when I got depressed,
The boys all biceps and the girls all chest,
Their comic Ford, their farm where I could be
"Really myself." I'll show you, come to that,
The bracken where I never trembling sat,
Determined to go through with it; where she
Lay back, and "all became a burning mist."
And, in those offices, my doggerel
Was not set up in blunt ten-point, nor read
By a distinguished cousin of the mayor,
Who didn't call and tell my father There
Before us, had we the gift to see ahead—
"You look as though you wished the place in Hell,"
My friend said, "judging from your face." "Oh well,
I suppose it's not the place's fault," I said.

"Nothing, like something, happens anywhere."

A Ford and a farm, some bracken and some doggerel: even the
past the speaker didn't have was boring. The thought of these

banal deprivations hurtles him into abstract extremity: anyone, anywhere might have not have been cast down by these biceped boys and breasted girls, might not have had his doggerel set up in blunt ten-point type. "I Remember, I Remember" is the title of a sentimental poem by the nineteenth-century poet Thomas Hood; its final lines are, "I'm farther off from heav'n / Than when I was a boy." But you don't need to know Hood's poem to know that Larkin is a godless Job, near no heaven.

Now, comic—a wistful caprice, a garland of sweet nothings by Troy Jollimore:

> Regret
> I'd like to take back my not saying to you
> those things that, out of politeness, or caution,
> I kept to myself. And, if I may—
> though this might perhaps stretch the rules—I'd like
> to take back *your* not saying some of the things
> that you never said, like "I love you" and "Won't you
> come home with me," or telling me, which
> you in fact never did, perhaps in the newly
> refurbished café at the Vancouver Art
> Gallery as fresh drops of the downpour from which
> we'd sought shelter glinted in your hair like jewels,
> or windshields of cars as seen from a plane
> that has just taken off or is just coming in
> for a landing, when the sun is at just the right angle,
> that try as you might, you could not imagine
> a life without me. The passionate spark

that would have flared up in your eye as you said this—
if you had said this—I dream of it often.
I won't take those back, those dreams, though I would,
if I could, take back your not kissing me, openly,
extravagantly, not caring who saw,
or those looks of anonymous animal longing
you'd throw everyone else in the room. I'd like
to retract my retracting, just before I grabbed you,
my grabbing you on the steps of the New York
Public Library (our failure to visit
which I would also like to recall)
and shouting for all to hear, "You, you
and only you!" Yes, I'd like to take back
my not frightening the pigeons that day with my wild
protestations of uncontrolled love, my not scaring
them off into orbit, frantic and mad,
even as I now sit alone, frantic and mad,
racing to unread the book of our love
before you can finish unwriting it.

The Vancouver Art Museum, newly refurbished; the fresh drops
of rain; the hair, the jewels, the windshields, cars, planes ascending
and descending, the sun at just the right angle, the spark that
flares in her eye, the kiss, the wild protestations, the frantic, mad
pigeons. Scenes imagined, ever-more obsessively itemized, more
brightly colored, as the speaker orbits into his unled life. It's as if
getting all the particulars exactly right would turn reverie into
memory, as if precision could guarantee truth. But Jollimore
writes, as it were, with his eraser. For it wasn't only in the Vancouver Art Museum that this woman didn't tell him that she

couldn't live without him, not only in its café, and not only when the museum was refurbished. She did not tell him sheltered from the rain or watching a plane, she did not tell him here or there, she did not tell him anywhere.

———

Thomas Hardy lived a long life in this emotional landscape, sober and comical, where misty abstractions settle on earthy particulars. He described distinctively tortured characters and asked us to take them as representative of human existence in general—of Life and Man. We are, as he put it in the title of one of his poetry collections, *Time's Laughingstocks,* the phrase characteristically juxtaposing the grandly abstract with the ludicrous particular. He finds inordinate pleasure and inordinate unhappiness in constructing pretentions to topple. As William Empson remarks, "Hardy is fond of showing us an unusually stupid person subjected to very unusually bad luck, and then a moral is drawn, not merely by inference but by solemn assertion, that we are all in the same boat as this person whose story is striking precisely because it is unusual." It can be maddening. Tess slips a hopeful envelope under her lover's door, Hardy nudges it under the carpet, I go see what's in the refrigerator.

Woolf heard this note in Hardy's novels, too, but her response was more generous than Empson's and less cringing than mine. Hardy's characters, she said, "live as individuals and they differ as individuals; but they also live as types and have a likeness as types." They're exceptional and anybody, particular and general. But Woolf then goes on to enter Hardy's way of thinking and, in doing so, she sustains and amplifies the beauty within it:

We see, as if it existed alone and for all time, the wagon with Fanny's dead body inside travelling along the road under the dripping trees; we see the bloated sheep struggling among the clover; we see Troy flashing his sword around Bathsheba where she stands motionless, cutting the lock off her head and splitting the caterpillar on her breast. Vivid to the eye, but not to the eye alone, for every sense participates, such scenes dawn upon us and their splendor remains.

Each of us is merely one among many, no different, really, from the rest. Yet Woolf sees that this truth needn't desolate us. Each scene, each character, each action is also particular and vivid, enduringly present in Hardy's writing and in her memory: this wagon beneath these dripping trees; this caterpillar, open on Bathsheba's breast.

The day's milking is over and Tess walks in a ragged garden at the dairy, beneath Angel Clare's window. In the soundless, foreshortened evening everything seems to approach and touch her. Pollen floats across her face, the rank weeds dampen her skirts, thistle milk and slug slime stain her pale, naked arms, snail shells crack into the soft underside of her feet. When the sound of Clare's harp descends through the still, silent air, it comes to her "with a stark quality like that of nudity." Tess's garden seems to leave its stain on me, too. *This* has happened, it happened here, and needn't have happened at all. Yes, nothing happens anywhere; but, then again, something— some particular thing—happens somewhere. For a moment, what might have happened drops away, and we're left lingering with what has happened in this one radiant world, with snail

shells denting our feet, and the descent of music into our neglected garden.

———

It's no wonder that Woolf heard this music in Hardy's novels:
it's there in her writing, too. In almost everything she wrote—
from her first short story, through the diaries she kept and the
novels she published, to the last note she left for her husband—
other lives lived with her. Her marriage, her childlessness, her
sisterhood, her survival of those she loved (and those she didn't
love much), her career: she understood all these not always but
often by comparing her lot with others'. It could be devastating.
"For God's sake, don't compare," she once wrote in her diary, as
if she couldn't help herself. And perhaps she couldn't. Read
enough of her, and comparison can seem to be a part of who she
is, inextricable from how she feels and thinks. Inextricable, too,
from how she writes.

"I do not know how far I differ from other people," she remarks
in one of her memoirs.

> Yet to describe oneself truly one must have some standard
> of comparison; was I clever, stupid, good looking, ugly,
> passionate, cold—? Owing partly to the fact that I was
> never at school, never competed in any way with children
> of my own age, I have never been able to compare my gifts
> and defects with other people's.

Without others, Woolf suggests, she has no words. But she
must be overstating matters. While it's true that school teaches
comparison, we can learn the skill elsewhere—for instance, in
the family. And as an adult living in in Bloomsbury, Woolf

found an extended set of peers with whom she compared herself relentlessly. So, how are we to understand her claim that she can't compare her gifts and defects with others'? I think it expresses its opposite: not that she has never been able to start comparing herself with others, but that she has never been able to stop—she can't compare conclusively and thus bring comparison, and thus description, to rest. Unlike others, she says, I can't compare.

Comparison led Woolf to desire another world. Not to desire that world rather than this one, but to desired it in addition to this one. Not this *instead* of that, but this *and* that. Her desire for another world came, I think, from her love of this one.

"Either we are men, or we are women," Woolf writes in *Jacob's Room*. "Either we are cold, or we are sentimental. Either we are young, or growing old"; we live as types and have likenesses as types. Classifying and comparing, shuttling through abstract categories, we drain the world of color and substance. "Life is but a procession of shadows," she writes, "and God knows why it is that we embrace them so eagerly, and see them depart with such anguish, being shadows."

> If this and much more than this is true, why are we yet surprised in the window corner by a sudden vision that the young man in the chair is of all things in the world the most real, the most solid, the best known to us—why indeed? For the moment after we know nothing about him.

> Such is the manner of our seeing. Such the conditions of our love.

It's the rhythm of the passage that undoes me: the steady procession of lightly punctuated, puzzling phrases comes to a rest,
and I rest with it. After that movement, what's wanted, and for a
perfect moment given, is this young man in this chair, real, solid,
known and alone, seen and tenderly held.

From the start, I've noticed the way meaning can be carried
elsewhere than in words. It was lodged between the "I" and
the "I" in "The Road Not Taken," for instance, and in the syn-
tactic outcroppings of "Easter Morning." It was there in the
fact that Jimmy Stewart and George Bailey were and were not
the same person. It was there in the silence that surrounded
Andrea del Sarto's nocturne. Here, in Woolf's writing, meaning
comes in the rhythm of her phrase; she's on a reach, then, suddenly, all sails are slack. Sometimes a sentence or paragraph
will have this rhythm, sometimes an entire novel. Woolf can
scale it up and scale it down. But whatever the scale of her
movement, it carries with it a feeling of unspoken simplicity
and profound fondness like that Woolf feels for the young
man in his chair.

   As she walks through the fresh morning air to buy flowers for
her evening party, Clarissa Dalloway begins to imagine another
life for herself: "Oh, if she could have had her life over again! she
thought, stepping on to the pavement, could have looked even differently!" Before her errand is over, Clarissa has imagined being
like Lady Boxborough, slow, stately, and large; has imagined a life
in which she could love the unlovable Miss Kilmann; and
imagined one in which she is like her husband, someone who
does things for himself. Clarissa is so ready to imagine other lives
for herself that she can later conjure a world of pleasure from the
gormless Peter Walsh. "All in a clap it came over her" as she sits

with him side by side on the sofa: "If I had married him, this gaiety would have been mine all day!"

London is in movement. Its bright lights and high clouds slide overhead, and its people bustle past. Clarissa's thoughts are on the move, too. Woolf's writing conveys all this movement, its flicker and flow, and then releases it.

> Heaven only knows why one loves it so, how one sees it so, making it up, building it round one, tumbling it, creating it every moment afresh; but the veriest frumps, the most dejected of miseries sitting on doorsteps (drink their downfall) do the same; can't be dealt with by Acts of Parliament for that very reason; they love life. In people's eyes, in the swing, tramp, and trudge; in the bellow and the uproar; the carriages, motor cars, omnibuses, vans, sandwich men shuffling and swinging; brass bands; barrel organs; in the triumph and the jungle and the strange high singing of some aeroplane overhead was what she loved; life. London; this moment of June.

This swelling of tension and relaxation into simplicity describes the rhythm of the novel as a whole, starting as it does with Clarissa's morning plunge into the clamor of London, its sunlit energy and movement, the cars and cloud-writing plane, the subway, steam rising and swirling, Clarissa and Peter and Richard and Rezia and Septimus threading their separate ways through the city, traced all the while by the narrator, gliding from person to person, the whole finally growing to greatest energy in the party itself, where all our central characters have gathered and circulate from room to room. Then, as the party fades into a serene early morning, Woolf comes to her climax and her novel's end. Peter sits alone, and asks himself questions:

What is this terror? What is this ecstasy? he thought to himself. What is it that fills me with extraordinary excitement?

It is Clarissa, he said.

For there she was.

It's audacious, really, to end a novel so quietly. Woolf again sets her simple sentences apart on the page, formatted here as if poetry, each its own paragraph. And again, it's the rhythm of the sentences that carries the force of the feeling. The present settles into the past, "is" into "was," as our reading of the novel enters our past. Woolf withdraws herself and her words as far as she can in order to leave us with the simple presence of the world.

––––––––

We're used to trompe l'oeil, when paintings tease us with reality. The saint's foot edges beyond its pedestal and toes the air around us, the nobleman holds out a ring to us, a man, smoking, leans out of his window and into the museum. But sometimes the movement goes the other direction. It's not that art enters our space, but that we enter its. We act a role or speak in meter, we see someone standing contrapposto against a wall, or watch a boy walk down the street, seeming, for a moment, to dance. We're graced by the artistry of what is—another form of trompe l'oeil.

––––––––

In Woolf's diaries you can hear her finding her rhythm of withdrawal in everyday life. It's Boxing Day, 1929. She has had her old friend Clive Bell to tea. For an hour or two they've sat together and talked about her novels and his love affairs, and about the nature of love itself; they've communed within their long intimacy. An ordinary afternoon of talk; two old friends turn over the past between them. Suddenly a third figure looms: Woolf's brother, Clive's old friend, Thoby, who died young, decades earlier. He's a "queer ghost," Woolf writes, present in the room and not present, familiar and unfamiliar, within her memory and outside of her. His appearance sends her back to think about herself, about the life she's led since his death. A second image comes to her, the image of her own life, ended. It's the most moving moment in all the decades of her diaries, a spontaneous, elegiac movement of her heart, and it's marked with the same falling gentleness we've heard in her novels. Talk and restless movement subside into quiet, familiar simplicity: "I think of [my] death," she writes, "sometimes as the end of an excursion which I went on when he died. As if I should come in & say, well, here you are."

————

Such is the manner of our seeing.
It is Clarissa, he said.
For there she was.
Well, here you are.

Like most teachers of writing I tell my students to avoid the verb "to be"—to avoid "is," "are," "was," "were." "Give me real verbs!" I shout at them. "What does 'is' tell you, what does 'are' tell you? Nothing! Merely that something exists!" It was only this year, after saying this for a quarter century, that it occurred to me to add, "Well, nothing and everything, I suppose."

Circling back, returning, recalling, going back down the ways of the past, reading and reading again: if that habit of mind has suited stories of our unled lives, and suited me, writing about them, so too has an impulse simply to stop and see. Really, it's become the stronger impulse. I dream of a book composed solely of quotations, as if I were simply to say, "There it is." As if I could simply point.

Prayer

GALWAY KINNELL

Whatever happens. Whatever
what is is is what
I want. Only that. But that.

Yes. But only if we remember that *what is* includes our strange ability to see what is not, as we see the moon shining with a light not its own. Who knows this better than poets? And who knows better than poets that this strange ability is a burden as well as a gift? That's why Kinnell must pray.

It is 1926, the year after *Mrs. Dalloway* was published. Woolf is describing her day in her diary.

Then (as I was walking through Russell Sqre last night) I see the mountains in the sky: the great clouds; & the moon which is risen over Persia; I have a great & astonishing sense of something there, which is "it"—It is not exactly beauty that I mean. It is that the thing is in itself enough: satisfactory; achieved.

And with that sense of something achieved, satisfactory, set apart from her, comes a changed experience of herself: "A sense of my own strangeness, walking on the earth is there too: of the oddity of the human position; trotting along Russell Sqre with the moon up there, & those mountain clouds." In its way, this passage is as powerful a description of the reception of the world as I could want. Woolf is testifying to the wonder and strangeness of simple facts. "The thing is in itself enough." Other worlds fall away to leave this one: the clouds and the moon in the sky above her. A view not down from elevated indifference—not sub species aeternitatis—but up from this strange earth.

And yet, in these moments in which the thing in itself is enough, satisfactory, achieved, the thought of what is not hasn't been eliminated. Woolf holds enough and longing together with a human inconsistency, sometimes feeling one, sometimes the other and—this is her genius—sometimes both together. In the sky she sees the clouds that are there and the mountains that are not. And the moon? It may seem that she simply points to it. But, she says, as it shines here down on Russell Square in London, it also shines on Persia—where her lover, Vita Sackville West, had sailed a few months earlier. The moon is here and there, on Woolf and the woman she loves: it is one traveler on two roads.

If this isn't beauty, it's more than beauty; it's beauty and heartbreak together. Regret and relief may be the most familiar signs of our unled lives, but this heartbreaking beauty is the most moving to me. It's the freedom and the loneliness of middle age.

———

I think back to what Blanchot said about the radiance of Henry James's stories, that they both provide an entire work and make its unrealized possibilities present, "the infinite and light space

of the narrative as it could have been, as it is before any beginning." James's writing introduced me to this mixed beauty, as
Woolf's writing now help me to my end. She receives the world
in her language and in so doing, testifies to it; she makes moving
the reception of what is, even as she acknowledges what is not.
Because no one else carries that beauty with her grace, I'm tempted
to stop here. But the note Woolf sounded a century ago can still
be heard. Indeed, in this day of careening sociality and image
flow, her rhythm of headlong movement and sudden, astonished
attention is a familiar feature of daily life.

Here, for instance, is the poet Mark Doty, in New York City:
"A sharp cracking cold day, the air of the Upper East Side full of
rising plumes of smoke from furnaces and steaming laundries,
exhaust from the tailpipes of idling taxis, flapping banners, gangs
of pigeons." He's spent the morning in the Metropolitan Museum.
It's been very crowded inside and out. The museum steps have
been "alive all day with commerce and hurry, with gatherings and
departures." But for Doty, as he stands in the cold, the busy
scene is suffused with warmth. He's seen a particular still life in
the museum, *Still Life with Oysters and Lemon* by Jan Davidsz
de Heem, and it pulled him deeply into its stillness. He remains
in its mood. "The overall effect," he writes, "the result of looking
and looking into its brimming surface as long as I could look, is
love, by which I mean a sense of tenderness towards experience,
of being held within an intimacy with the things of the world."
For this moment, the world, too, brims. There's more in it than
words can say.

To end this book, then, I'll glance at two recent writers of unled
lives who capture this rhythm and the profound, tender simplicity
it brings in its train. They each turn the collection of our themes
their own way, varying them, emphasizing this aspect or that.

They make what they will of familiar words, and so create something new.

———

Jenny Offill's *Dept. of Speculation* is composed of elliptical paragraphs, isolated events of blank-faced factual documentation, phrases bitten off rather than written.

> For years, I kept a Post-it note above my desk. WORK NOT LOVE was what it said. It seemed a sturdier kind of happiness.

> I found a book called *Thriving Not Surviving* in a box on the street. I stood there, flipping through it, unwilling to commit.

As these statements accumulate, you begin to get a sense of the narrator. She's a young New Yorker. Her closest friend is a philosopher. She's a fact-checker at a science magazine. She has a side job as a researcher for a rich man who's writing a memoir about not quite becoming an astronaut. ("The almost astronaut calls me at all hours now to talk about his project. 'I think it's going to be a best seller,' he tells me. 'Like that guy. What's his name? Sagan?'") She once planned to be an unmarried artist, an "art monster," as she put it. "That night," she says, "I bring up my old art monster plan. 'Road not taken,' my husband says."

Slowly, a story of career and marriage and the beginnings of family life takes shape. It's a story littered with debris.

> When we first saw the apartment, we were excited that it had a yard but disappointed that the yard was filled by a

large jungle gym that we didn't need. Later, when we signed
the lease, we were happy about the jungle gym because I'd
learned that I was pregnant and we could imagine its uses.
But by the time we moved in, we had found out that the
baby's heart had stopped and now it just made us sad to
look out the window at it.

The narrator becomes pregnant again and has a daughter. Her
husband has an affair.

It is easy in retrospect to see why he'd want to go. There
are two women who are furious at him. To make one happy
he must take the subway across town and arrive on her
doorstep. To make the other happy, he must wear for some
infinitely long period of time a hair shirt woven out of her
own hair.

Either the narrator is an unmarried artist, or she is a married
fact-checker. Either she is a mother, or she is not a mother. Either
her husband stays with her or he doesn't. But life is less stark than
this. Boundaries blur. After the narrator has a miscarriage, is she a
mother? Is she a fact-checker or the author of a fact-checkered
novel? When her husband has an affair, are they no longer married? Are she and her husband two separate people or joined as
one? That question at least gets an answer: "At night, they lie in bed
holding hands. It is possible if she is stealthy enough that the wife
can do this while secretly giving the husband the finger." But most
of the narrator's questions can't be answered so perfectly. She strug-
gles to say what she needs to say. She tests syntax: "The wife has
never not wanted to be married to him. This sounds false but it is
true." And diction: "The wife thinks the old word is better. She says
he is *besotted*. The shrink says he is *infatuated*. She doesn't want to

tell what the husband says." And narrative convention: the book starts in the first person, switches to third when the wife discovers her husband's adultery, and returns to first when he returns.

But through this broken language, the pain of living with all that has happened and all that hasn't happened and all that can't happen is lit by sly wonders. We're brought to feel not that in its transience this experience might disappear, but that in its singularity it might never have been. Their daughter has broken her arm. It's hot, her cast itches, and she's miserable.

> One night we let her sleep in our room because the air conditioner is better. We all pile into the big bed. There is a musty animal smell to her casts now. She brings in the nightlight that makes fake stars and places it on the bedside table. Soon everyone is asleep but me. I lie in our bed and listen to the hum of the air conditioner and the soft sound of their breathing. Amazing. Out of dark waters, this.

The narrator receives this inexplicable intimacy as it is. She lets it imprint itself on the page, like a watermark. Past tense becomes present in the night, and verbs drift away with the memories of the day. No action now, no plot: time is suspended in soft sound. Even "to be" would disturb the still fulfillment of her sleepiness. "Out of dark waters, this."

———————

The story goes that the painter Pierre Bonnard was arrested in the Louvre, paintbrush and palette in hand, standing before one of his own paintings, reconsidering, retouching, continuing, reconsidering, retouching again: busily extending his look to eternity. He dreamt of paintings forever unfinished and of life as one long day of vernissage. Jane Hirshfield's poem "History as the Painter

Bonnard" sustains this fantasy—shares and studies this desire to see and see again—starting with its unfinished first line:

> Because nothing is ever finished
> the painter would shuffle, *bonnarding,*
> into galleries, museums, even the homes of his patrons,
> with hidden palette and brush:
> overscribble drapery and table with milk jug or fattened
>   pear,
> the clabbered, ripening colors of second sight.
> Though he knew with time the pentimenti rise—

Pierre Bonnard, *Woman with Basket of Fruit,* 1915–1918, Baltimore Museum of Art

half-visible, half brine-swept fish, their plunged shapes
pocking the mind—toward the end, only revision
    mattered:
to look again, more deeply, harder, clearer,
the one redemption granted us to ask.
This, we say, is what we meant to say. This. This.
—as the kiss, the sorrowful murmur,
may cover a child's bruises, if not retract the blow.

The first three lines are tetrameter and fairly fleet; even the long third line has only four heavily stressed syllables, and the fourth but three. But when we start up again after the colon and line break, we find in the next line seven or eight stresses, and in the stanza's last line almost every word carries a stress. "The clabbered, ripening colors of second sight": my ears catch the thickening of the poem's facture, the forced ripeness of the language. This is an overscribbled and clabbered line, gouts of words after the poem's thin opening phrases.

In interviews, Hirshfield has said that "History as the Painter Bonnard" was prompted by the 1989 Velvet Revolution in Czechoslovakia. She found herself unable to comprehend what was happening so far away. All she knew was that her first responses to those historical events were too simple. "Then," she says, "I thought of Bonnard." As she worked on the poem she evidently thought more and more about Bonnard, for he takes it over. The revolution is nowhere to be seen. It's the poem's overscribbled underdrawing; only as we move toward the conclusion does it swim upward and in two lines break the surface before diving back below:

while a woman in Prague asks softly, in good English,
    for the camera, "But who will give us back these twenty
    years?"

Ah love, o history, forgive
the squandered light and flung-down rags of chances,
old choices drifted terribly awry.

And world, self-portrait never right, receive this gift—
shuffling, spattered, stubborn,
something nameless opens in the heart: to touch
with soft-bent sable, ground-earth pigment, seed-clear
    oil,
the rounding, bright-fleshed present, if not the past.

The kissed child puts his hand at last back into his
    mother's,
though it is not the same;
her fine face neither right nor wrong, only thoroughly
    his.

Nothing is the same; the blow cannot be retracted. Hirshfield's poem is about the desire to return, and the nature of that desire. Who will give you back your past? Not the gods, nor narrators, nor poets or painters. The past is irrevocable, and each of your moments excludes all others, even as this person is not that, even as this child is not his mother in whom he once was, whose hand he at last holds.

All you can do is try to see the bright-fleshed present truly, and in seeing, join it. If this was Bonnard's fantasy, Hirshfield shares it. Nothing is ever finished. Pentimenti rise through paint; fish surface on an evening lake; bruises bloom upward through skin. We live in the presence of something meaningful, but don't possess it. And so, we look hard, deeply, and let something nameless open in the heart; we pause and then try to paint it clearly, to touch it with repeated dabs of words: "This, This," we say. *This.*

Nothing is of greater moment than the knowledge that the choice of one moment excludes another, that no moment makes up for another, that the significance of one moment is the cost of what it forgoes. That is refinement. Beauty and significance, except in youth, are born of loss. But otherwise everything is lost. The last knowledge will be to allow even that knowledge of loss to vanish, to see whether the world regains. The idea of infinite possibility is the pain, and the balm, of adolescence. The only return on becoming adult, the only justice in forgoing that world of possibility, is the reception of actuality—the pain and the balm in the truth of the only world: that it exists, and I in it.

—STANLEY CAVELL, THE WORLD VIEWED

WORKS CONSULTED

Not wanting to clutter the text with notes but wanting to make it easy for readers to pursue their interests further, I've compiled this list of works consulted. I've also listed several essays I've written that explore related ideas in more depth than I could here.

A few books have been generally helpful. I encourage readers wanting to think more about our unled lives to read the work of Gary Saul Morson and Michael André Bernstein. Morson's essay was especially helpful in getting me to see the importance of the aesthetic standard I discuss early on. In *Foregone Conclusions* Bernstein discusses one topic I'm especially conscious of not treating: narratives of the Holocaust. Hilary Dannenberg's *Coincidence and Counterfactuality* provides a history of counterfactual narratives, analyzes their rhetorical functions, and describes their relation to coincidence. Catherine Gallagher's *Telling It Like It Wasn't* is a thorough study of counterfactual history and historical novels. The writing of Daniel Kahneman and his collaborators on counterfactuals is accessible, but Ruth Byrne's book *The Rational Imagination* is an incisive summary of subsequent psychological studies. Although I don't often refer to it, Stanley Cavell's writing in *The Claim of Reason* and *Conditions Handsome and Unhandsome* stands behind much of what I've written here. Finally, the essays collected in Adam Phillips's *Missing Out* and James Wood's *The Nearest Thing to Life* both speak engagingly to what we are not.

Preface

Baker, Nicholson. *The Anthologist*. New York: Simon & Schuster, 2009.

Barnes, Julian. *Flaubert's Parrot*. New York: Alfred A. Knopf, 1985.

———. *The Sense of an Ending*. New York: Alfred A. Knopf, 2011.

Browner, Jesse. *How Did I Get Here?: Making Peace with the Road Not Taken: A Memoir*. New York: Harper, 2015.

Cunningham, Michael. *The Hours*. New York: Farrar, Straus and Giroux, 1998.

Cusk, Rachel. *A Life's Work: On Becoming a Mother*. New York: Picador USA, 2002.

45 Years. Directed by Andrew Haigh. Film4 Productions, British Film Institute, Creative England, The Bureau, 2015.

Frost, Robert. "The Road Not Taken." In *Collected Poems, Prose & Plays*. New York: Library of America, 1995.

Hall, Tom T. "Pamela Brown." *We All Got Together and . . .*, Mercury Records, 1972.

Kundera, Milan. *The Unbearable Lightness of Being*. New York: Harper & Row, 1984.

While We're Young. Directed by Noah Baumbach. Scott Rudin Productions, 2014.

Williams, Bernard. "Imagination and the Self." In *Problems of the Self: Philosophical Papers 1956–1972*. Cambridge: Cambridge University Press, 1973.

Woolf, Virginia. *The Waves*. New York: Harcourt Brace Jovanovich, 1978.

Introduction

Austen, Jane. *Emma*. Oxford: Oxford University Press, 1998.

Blanchot, Maurice. *The Book to Come*. Translated by Charlotte Mandell. Stanford, CA: Stanford University Press, 2003.

Defoe, Daniel. *Robinson Crusoe*. Oxford: Oxford University Press, 2009.

Dickens, Charles. *Bleak House*. New York: W. W. Norton, 1977.

———. *A Christmas Carol and Other Christmas Books*. Oxford: Oxford University Press, 2006.

———. *David Copperfield*. Oxford: Oxford University Press, 1999.

———. *Great Expectations*. Oxford: Clarendon Press, 1993.

Eliot, George. *Middlemarch*. New York: Penguin, 2003.

Eliot, T. S. *The Use of Poetry and Use of Criticism*. Cambridge, MA: Harvard University Press, 1986.

Empson, William. *Some Versions of Pastoral*. New York: New Directions Pub. Corp., 1968.

Ferrante, Elena. *Neapolitan Novels*. New York: Europa Editions, 2012–2015.

Freud, Sigmund. "On Transience." In *The Collected Works of Sigmund Freud*, vol. 14, edited by James Strachey. London: Hogarth Press, 1957.

Frost, Robert. "The Road Not Taken." In *Collected Poems, Prose & Plays*. New York: Library of America, 1995.

Geertz, Clifford. *The Interpretation of Cultures: Selected Essays*. New York: Basic Books, 1973.

Goodman, Paul. *The Structure of Literature*. Chicago: University of Chicago Press, 1954.

Gordon, Mary. *The Love of My Youth*. New York: Pantheon Books, 2011.

Hardy, Thomas. *Jude the Obscure*. Oxford: Oxford University Press, 2008.

———. *The Mayor of Casterbridge*. New York: Penguin, 2018.

———. *Tess of the D'Urbervilles*. New York: Penguin, 2003.

Hurston, Zora Neal. *Passing*. New York: Penguin, 2003.

James, Henry. *The Ambassadors*. New York: Penguin, 2006.

———. "The Jolly Corner." In *Complete Stories, 1898–1910*, 697–731. New York: Library of America, 1996.

———. "Diary of a Man of Fifty." In *Complete Stories, 1874–1884*. New York: Library of America, 1999.

———. "The Prefaces to the New York Edition." In *Literary Criticism: European Writers and the Prefaces*, 1035–1343. New York: Library of America, 1984.

———. "The Private Life." In *Complete Stories, 1892–1898*. New York: Library of America, 1996.

Lamb, Charles. "Oxford at the Vacation." *London Magazine* 2 (October 1820): 365–369.

McCann, Colum. *Let the Great World Spin*. New York: Random House, 2009.

Phillips, Adam. *Darwin's Worms.* New York: Basic Books, 2000.

———. *Missing Out: In Praise of the Unlived Life.* New York: Farrar, Straus and Giroux, 2013.

Poulet, Georges. *Metamorphoses of the Circle.* Baltimore, MD: Johns Hopkins University Press, 1967.

Rilke, Rainer M. *Duino Elegies and the Sonnets to Orpheus.* Translated by C. F. MacIntyre. Berkeley: University of California Press, 2001.

Roese, Neal J., and James N. Olson. "Counterfactual Thinking: A Critical Overview." In *What Might Have Been: The Social Psychology of Counterfactual Thinking,* edited by Neal J. Roese and James N. Olson, 1–56. Mahwah, NJ: Lawrence Erlbaum Associates, 1995.

Roth, Phillip. *The Counterlife.* New York: Vintage Books, 1996.

———. *Operation Shylock: A Confession.* New York: Vintage Books, 1994.

Shriver, Lionel. *The Post-Birthday World.* New York: HarperCollins Publishers, 2007.

Sontag, Susan. "On Style." In *Essays of the 1960s & 1970s,* 21–43. New York: Library of America, 2013.

Stevens, Wallace. "Sunday Morning." In *Wallace Stevens: Collected Poetry and Prose.* New York: Library of America, 2003.

Wilde, Oscar. "L'envoi." In *Miscellanies,* 30–41. London: Methuen, 1908.

Woloch, Alex. *The One vs. the Many.* Princeton, NJ: Princeton University Press, 2003.

Woolf, Virginia. *The Diary of Virginia Woolf.* 5 volumes. New York: Harvest Books, 1977.

———. *Mrs. Dalloway.* New York: Mariner Books, 1990.

———. *The Waves.* New York: Harcourt Brace Jovanovich, 1978.

1. One Person, Two Roads

Aristotle. *The Nicomachean Ethics.* Translated by David Ross. Oxford: Oxford University Press, 2009.

Auden, W. H. "Musée des Beaux Arts." In *Collected Poems.* New York: Random House, 1968.

Austen, Jane. *Persuasion.* New York: W. W. Norton, 2013.

Benjamin, Walter. "On The Image of Proust." In *Selected Writings*, vol. 2, 237–247. Cambridge, MA: The Belknap Press of Harvard University Press, 1996.

Browning, Robert. "Andrea del Sarto." In *Robert Browning, the Poems*. New Haven, CT: Yale University Press, 1981.

Bruegel, Pieter. *Landscape with the Fall of Icarus*. 1560, Royal Museums of Fine Arts of Belgium, Brussels.

———. *The Census at Bethlehem*.1566, Royal Museums of Fine Arts of Belgium, Brussels.

Butler, Joseph. *Five Sermons, Preached At the Rolls Chapel and A Dissertation Upon the Nature of Virtue*. Indianapolis, IN: Hackett, 1983.

Cavell, Stanley. "North by Northwest." In *Themes Out of School*. Chicago: University of Chicago Press, 1984.

———. *Pursuits of Happiness: The Hollywood Comedy of Remarriage*. Cambridge, MA: Harvard University Press, 1981.

Cheever, John. *The Journals of John Cheever*. New York: Alfred A. Knopf, 1991.

Cohen, Rachel, et al. "A Symposium on Bruegel." *Threepenny Review*, no. 121 (Spring 2010): 22–24.

Cohen, Ted. *Thinking of Others: On the Talent for Metaphor*. Princeton, NJ: Princeton University Press, 2008.

Dennis, Carl. "The God Who Loves You." In *Practical Gods*. New York: Penguin Poets, 2001.

Dickens, Charles. *A Christmas Carol and Other Christmas Books*. Oxford: Oxford University Press, 2006.

———. *David Copperfield*. Oxford: Oxford University Press, 1999.

———. *Great Expectations*. Oxford: Clarendon Press, 1993.

Dickens, Mamie. *My Father As I Recall Him*. New York: E. P. Dutton, 1896.

Dickinson, Emily. "Remorse—Is Memory—Awake." In *The Poems of Emily Dickinson*, edited by R. W. Franklin. Cambridge, MA: The Belknap Press of Harvard University Press, 1998.

Eliot, George. *Middlemarch*. Oxford: Oxford University Press, 1997.

———. *Selected Essays, Poems, and Other Writings*. New York: Penguin, 1991.

Empson, William. *Seven Types of Ambiguity*. New York: Meridian Books, 1955.

Empson, William, Bernard Heringman, and John Unterecker. "Three Critics on One Poem: Hart Crane's 'Voyages III.'" *Essays in Criticism* 46, no. 1 (January 1996): 16–27.

Ermarth, Elizabeth. *Realism and Consensus in the English Novel Consensus in the English Novel.* Princeton, NJ: Princeton University Press, 1983.

Fauset, Jesse Redmon. *Plum Bun.* Philadelphia, PA: Oshun Publishing Company, 2013.

Forster, John. *The Life of Charles Dickens.* London: Chapman and Hall, 1873.

Goodman, Nelson. "The Problem of Counterfactual Conditionals." *Journal of Philosophy* 44, no. 5 (1947): 113–128.

Hardy, Thomas. *Far From the Madding Crowd.* New York: Penguin, 2003.

Hazlitt, William. "On Personal Identity." In *Selected Writings.* Oxford: Oxford University Press, 2009.

Holiday, Billie. "I'll be Seeing You." *The Complete Commodore / Decca Masters.* Sammy Fain and Irving Kahal, Hip-O Records, 2009.

Hume, David. *Treatise of Human Nature.* Oxford: Clarendon Press, 1973.

It's a Wonderful Life. Directed by Frank Capra. Republic Entertainment, 1998.

James, Henry. "Diary of a Man of Fifty." In *Complete Stories, 1874–1884.* New York: Library of America, 1999.

———. Letter to Alice James, 8 April 1877. In *Henry James, A Life in Letters,* edited by Philip Horne, 87. New York: Penguin, 1999.

———. "The Private Life." In *Complete Stories, 1892–1898.* New York: Library of America, 1996.

Jarrell, Randall. "Next Day." In *The Complete Poems.* New York: Farrar, Straus and Giroux, 1969.

Kahneman, Daniel, and Dale T. Miller. "Norm Theory: Comparing Reality to Its Alternatives." *Psychological Review* 93, no. 2 (1986): 136–153.

Kahneman, Daniel, and Amos Tversky. "The Simulation Heuristic." In *Judgment Under Uncertainty: Heuristics and Biases,* edited by Daniel Kahneman, Paul Slovic, and Amos Tversky, 201–211. Cambridge: Cambridge University Press, 1982.

Larkin, Philip. *Collected Poems.* New York: Farrar, Straus and Giroux, 1989.

———. *A Girl in Winter*. London: Faber & Faber, 2005.

Lewis, David. "Causation." *Journal of Philosophy* 70, no. 17 (1973): 556–567.

Lewis, David Levering. *When Harlem Was in Vogue*. New York: Penguin, 1997.

Lewis, Michael. "My Ames Is True." *This American Life*, from WBEZ, September 6, 2013. https://www.thisamericanlife.org/504/how-i-got -into-college/act-two-5.

Letter from an Unknown Woman. Directed by Max Ophüls. Universal Pictures, 1948.

Mantel, Hilary. *Giving Up the Ghost: A Memoir*. New York: Henry Holt, 2003.

Morgan, Dan. "Max Ophüls and the Limits of Virtuosity: On the Aesthetics and Ethics of Camera Movement." *Critical Inquiry* 38 (Autumn 2011): 127–163.

Musil, Robert. *The Man Without Qualities*. Translated by Eithne Wilkins and Ernst Kaiser London: Secker & Warburg, 1953.

Nietzsche, Friedrich Wilhelm. *The Gay Science: With a Prelude in German Rhymes and an Appendix of Songs*. Cambridge: Cambridge University Press, 2001.

Oliver, King. "Riverside Blues." *Louis Armstrong and King Oliver*. Milestone, 1992.

Pessoa, Fernando. "In the Terrible Night." In *A Little Larger Than the Entire Universe: Selected Poems*. Translated by Richard Zenith. New York: Penguin, 2003.

Rossetti, Daniel Gabriel. "Lost Days." In *Collected Poetry and Prose*. New Haven, CT: Yale University Press, 2003.

Roese, Neal. *If Only How to Turn Regret into Opportunity*. New York: Broadway Books, 2005.

Phillips, Adam. *Promises, Promises: Essays on Literature and Psychoanalysis*. New York: Basic Books, 2001.

Schuyler, James. "Salute." In *Collected Poems*. New York: Farrar, Straus and Giroux, 1993.

Stewart, Garrett. *Dear Reader: The Conscripted Audience in Nineteenth-Century Fiction*. Baltimore, MD: Johns Hopkins University Press, 1997.

Trollope, Anthony. *He Knew He Was Right*. Oxford: Oxford University Press, 1998.

Von Leibniz, Gottfried Wilhelm Freiherr. *Discourse on Metaphysics and Other Essays*. Translated by Roger Ariew and Daniel Garber. Indianapolis, IN: Hackett, 1991.

Williams, Bernard. "Imagination and the Self." In *Problems of the Self: Philosophical Papers 1956–1972*. Cambridge: Cambridge University Press, 1973.

Woolf, Virginia. *Mrs. Dalloway*. New York: Harcourt, Brace and Co., 1925.

———. *The Waves*. New York: Harcourt Brace Jovanovich, 1978.

2. Tales of Our Adulthood

Ammons, A. R. "Easter Morning." In *Collected Poems, 1951–1971*. New York: W. W. Norton, 1972.

Atkinson, Kate. *Life After Life: A Novel*. New York: Little, Brown and Company, 2013.

Auden, W. H. "Musée des Beaux-Arts." In *Collected Poems*. New York: Random House, 1976.

Baudelaire, Charles. *Paris Spleen, 1869*. Translated by Louise Varèse. New York: New Directions Pub. Corp., 1970.

Bidart, Frank. "For the AIDS Dead." In *Half-light: Collected Poems 1965–2016*. New York: Farrar, Straus and Giroux, 2017.

Brontë, Emily. *Wuthering Heights*. Oxford: Oxford University Press, 1998.

Brooks, Gwendolyn. "the mother." In *The Essential Gwendolyn Brooks*. New York: Library of America, 2005.

Carson, Anne. *Autobiography of Red*. New York: Vintage, 1998.

Cavell, Stanley. *The Claim of Reason: Wittgenstein, Skepticism, Morality, and Tragedy*. Oxford: Oxford University Press, 1999.

Davis, Lydia. *The Collected Stories of Lydia Davis*. New York: Farrar, Straus and Giroux, 2009.

Dickens, Charles. *Bleak House*. New York: W. W. Norton, 1977.

———. *Great Expectations*. Oxford: Clarendon Press, 1993.

Eliot, George. *Selected Essays, Poems, and Other Writings*. New York: Penguin, 1991.

Ferrante, Elena. *Neapolitan Novels*. New York: Europa Editions, 2012–2015.

Giddens, Anthony. *The Consequences of Modernity*. Stanford, CA: Stanford University Press, 1990.

Gordon, Mary. *The Love of My Youth*. New York: Pantheon Books, 2011.

Hardy, Thomas, *Complete Poems*. New York: Palgrave Macmillan, 2001.

———. *Far From the Madding Crowd*. New York: Penguin, 2003.

———. *Tess of the D'Urbervilles*. New York: Penguin, 2003

Hughes, Langston. "Passing." In *The Ways of White Folks*. New York: Vintage, 1990.

Ishiguro, Kazuo. *The Remains of the Day*. New York: Alfred A. Knopf, 1989.

James, William. "The Dilemma of Determinism." In *The Will to Believe. Writings, 1878–1899*, 445–704. New York: Library of America, 1992.

Jennings, Elizabeth. "For a Child Born Dead." In *Selected Poems*. Manchester, UK: Carcanet Press, 1980.

Johnson, James Weldon. *The Autobiography of an Ex-Colored Man*. New York: Penguin, 1990.

Kierkegaard, Søren. *The Sickness Unto Death*. Translated by Walter Lowrie. Princeton, NJ: Princeton University Press, 1941.

McEwan, Ian. *Atonement: A Novel*. New York: Anchor Books, 2003.

Messud, Claire. *The Woman Upstairs: A Novel*. New York: Alfred A. Knopf, 2013.

Mitchell, Juliet. *Siblings: Sex and Violence*. Hoboken, NJ: Wiley, 2013.

Nelson, Maggie. *The Argonauts*. Minneapolis, MN: Graywolf Press, 2015.

Nietzsche, Friedrich Wilhelm. *The Gay Science: With a Prelude in German Rhymes and an Appendix of Songs*. Translated by Josefine Nauckhoff and Adrian Del Caro. Cambridge: Cambridge University Press, 2001.

Olds, Sharon. *Stag's Leap*. New York: Alfred A. Knopf, 2012.

Peacock, Molly. "The Choice." *Poetry*, February, 1986, 266.

Perkin, Harold. *The Rise of Professional Society: England Since 1880*. New York: Routledge, 2002.

Phillips, Adam. *Monogamy*. New York: Pantheon Books, 1996.

Proulx, Annie. "Brokeback Mountain." In *Close Range: Wyoming Stories*. New York: Scribner, 1999.

Richardson, James. *Thomas Hardy: The Poetry of Necessity*. Chicago: University of Chicago Press, 1977.

Stanley, George. "Veracruz." In *A Tall, Serious Girl: Selected Poems 1957–2000*. New Britain, CT: Qua Books, 2003.

Schwartz, Barry. *The Paradox of Choice: Why More Is Less*. New York: ECCO, 2004.

Taylor, Charles. *Sources of the Self: The Making of the Modern Identity*. Cambridge, MA: Harvard University Press, 1989.

Updike, John. *Due Considerations: Essays and Criticism*. New York: Alfred A. Knopf, 2007.

West, Rebecca. *The Return of the Soldier*. New York: Penguin Books, 1998.

Wolitzer, Meg. *The Interestings*. New York: Riverhead Books, 2014.

Wood, Charles. "Mrs. Henry Wood: In Memoriam." *The Argosy* 43 (January–June 1887): 349.

Wood, Mrs. Henry. *East Lynne*. Oxford: Oxford University Press, 2005.

Woolf, Virginia. "Death of a Moth." In *Collected Essays*, vol. 1. New York: Harcourt Brace & World, 1950.

Zucker, Rachel. *The Pedestrians*. Seattle: Wave Books, 2014.

3. All the Difference

Blanchot, Maurice. *The Book to Come*. Translated by Charlotte Mandell. Stanford, CA: Stanford University Press, 2003.

Bonnard, Pierre. *Basket of Fruit*. 1924, The Baltimore Museum of Art, Baltimore.

Cavell, Stanley. *The World Viewed: Reflections on the Ontology of Film*. Cambridge, MA: Harvard University Press, 1979.

Dickens, Charles. *Great Expectations*. Oxford: Clarendon Press, 1993.

Doty, Mark. *Still Life with Oysters and Lemon*. Boston, MA: Beacon Press, 2001.

Empson, William. *The Strengths of Shakespeare's Shrew: Essays, Memoirs and Reviews*. Sheffield, England: Sheffield Academic Press, 1996.

Hardy, Thomas. *Far From the Madding Crowd*. New York: Penguin, 2003.

———. *Tess of the D'Urbervilles*. New York: Penguin, 2003.

Hirshfield, Jane. "History as the Painter Bonnard." In *The October Palace*. New York: Harper Collins, 1994.

———. "Zen and the Art of Poetry: An Interview with Jane Hirshfield." Interview by Ilya Kaminsky and Katherine Towler. *Agni Online,* January 30, 2018. https://agnionline.bu.edu/interview/zen-and-the-art -of-poetry-an-interview-with-jane-hirshfield.

Johnson, James Weldon. *The Autobiography of an Ex-Colored Man.* New York: Penguin, 1990.

Jollimore, Troy. "Regret." In *At Lake Scugog: Poems.* Princeton, NJ: Princeton University Press, 2011.

Kinnell, Galway. "Prayer." In *The Past.* New York: Houghton Mifflin Harcourt, 1985.

Larkin, Philip. *Collected Poems.* New York: Farrar, Straus and Giroux, 1989.

———. *A Girl in Winter.* London: Faber & Faber, 2005.

Nagel, Thomas. "The Absurd." *Journal of Philosophy* 68, no. 20 (1971): 716–727.

Offill, Jenny. *Dept. of Speculation.* New York: Alfred A. Knopf, 2014.

Woolf, Virginia. *The Diary of Virginia Woolf.* 5 vols. New York: Harvest Books, 1977.

———. *Jacob's Room.* New York: Harcourt Brace Jovanovich, 1978.

———. *Mrs. Dalloway.* New York: Harcourt, Brace and Co, 1925.

———. "The Novels of Thomas Hardy." In *Collected Essays,* vol. 1. New York: Harcourt Brace & World, 1950.

———. *A Writer's Diary: Being Extracts from the Diary of Virginia Woolf.* New York: Harcourt, Brace, 1954.

Further Reading

Bernstein, Michael A. *Foregone Conclusions: Against Apocalyptic History.* Berkeley: University of California Press, 1994.

Byrne, Ruth M. J. *The Rational Imagination: How People Create Alternatives to Reality.* Cambridge, MA: MIT Press, 2005.

Cavell, Stanley. *The Claim of Reason.* Oxford: Oxford University Press, 1979.

———. *Conditions Handsome and Unhandsome: The Constitution of Emersonian Perfectionism.* Chicago: University of Chicago Press, 1990.

————. *The Pursuits of Happiness*. Cambridge, MA: Harvard University Press, 1984.

Dannenberg, Hilary P. *Coincidence and Counterfactuality: Plotting Time and Space in Narrative Fiction*. Lincoln: University of Nebraska Press, 2008.

Gallagher, Catherine. "The Rise of Fictionality." In *The Novel*, edited by Franco Moretti, vol. 1, 336–363. Princeton, NJ: Princeton University Press, 2006.

————. *Telling It Like It Wasn't*. Chicago: University of Chicago Press, 2018.

Miller, Andrew H. "'A Case of Metaphysics': Counterfactuals, Realism, *Great Expectations*." *ELH* 79, no. 3 (Fall 2012): 773–796.

————. "*City Lights*: Five Scenes." *Raritan* 35, no. 1 (Summer 2015): 34–44.

————. "For All You Know." In *Stanley Cavell and Literary Studies: Consequences of Skepticism*, edited by Richard Eldridge and Bernie Ries, 194–207. London: Continuum Press, 2011.

————. "Lives Unled in Realist Fiction." *Representations* 98 (Spring 2007): 118–134.

————. "The One Cake, the Only Cake." *Michigan Quarterly Review* 51, no. 2 (Spring 2012): 167–186.

————. "Timepiece." *Brick* 93 (May 2014): 42–50.

Morson, Gary S. *Narrative and Freedom: The Shadows of Time*. New Haven, CT: Yale University Press, 1994.

Wood, James. *Nearest Thing to Life*. Lebanon, NH: Brandeis University Press, 2015.

ACKNOWLEDGMENTS

Writing this book has taken a long time, and I've asked for help from many people. I'm grateful to the audiences that have responded to my lectures and to the students who have discussed unled lives with me. Several friends and colleagues have read the manuscript as a whole, some of them more than once: Jim Adams, Cynthia Coffel-Miller, Jonathan Elmer, Mary Favret, Eileen Gillooly, Rae Greiner, Susan Gubar, Danny Hack, Ivan Krielkamp, Kieran Setiya, and Molly Young. Sungmey Lee and Sarah Ross provided important help at the end. First John Kulka, and then Lindsay Waters and Joy Deng at Harvard University Press were welcoming and supportive editors. Michael Gorra, Garry Hagberg, and three other, anonymous readers for the Press were sympathetic and acute.

Sophia, Cas, and Ben Miller were there at the start of this book and in different ways have encouraged me in the years since. Mary Favret helped me work through its ideas, kept me patient company as I wrote, and shared its burden. It's dedicated to her with love.

CREDITS

INDEX